THE NEXT
ECONOMY

PAUL
HAWKEN

BALLANTINE BOOKS • **NEW YORK**

Library of Congress Catalog Card Number: 82-23287

ISBN 0-345-31392-5

This edition published by arrangement with Holt, Rinehart and Winston

Manufactured in the United States of America

First Ballantine Books Edition: April 1984

TO PALO, ANASTASIA,
IONA, AND AIDAN

❇Contents

THE NEXT ECONOMY

❋ Introduction

Most people view the growing economic crises of the decade past as evidence of something gone wrong. Depending on one's economic philosophy, one can place the blame on various groups and institutions. Conservatives point to the government, monetarists blame the Federal Reserve Bank, Marxists blame the capitalist system, politicians blame their predecessors, consumers blame big business and OPEC, and big business has blamed consumers, OPEC, and government. Like a losing team, we see only our failure, and as a result, we have turned on one another.

Economic opinion has diverged because the economic events of the past decade do not fit into any economic theory. We are bewildered by an economy in which some suffer while others grow rich, in which some towns are worse off than they were during the Depression and others are booming. The economy de-

1

fies not only prognostication but categorization. Some things are working while others clearly are not. In 1981, 1982 and 1983 more businesses started up than at any other time in history. In 1982 and 1983 more businesses failed than at any time since the Depression.

There is another way to look at present economic events. We have entered a period between economies, or, to be more precise, between economic structures, and the troubled economy reflects the passage from one structure to the next. Current economic problems are no more a sign of failure than adolescence is the failure of childhood. While coming of age may not be the most apt metaphor for our crisis, it at least expresses the trauma that can accompany rapid change when proper understanding is lacking.

We are witnessing the relative decline of what I call the mass economy, the economy of the industrial age, a period during which nations amassed enormous manufacturing capabilities that depended on the large-scale extraction of resources, particularly fossil fuels. The mass economy was a *formative* economy in which virtually all of the work that human beings once did by hand or with the assistance of animals became mechanized through the use of machinery, technology, and energy. This mechanization included the development of the automobile, steel, rubber, chemical, electrical, heavy equipment, and machine tool industries as well as the thousands of businesses required to support them. Infusing the mass economy was what economist Robert Heilbroner calls the "thrusting, restive search of the participants . . . for their material advancement."

The success of the mass economy in producing a profligate amount of goods has in turn changed the formula for success. Energy, the resource that accomplishes most of the work in an industrial economy, is more expensive than it was ten, twenty, even one hundred years ago. Because it costs more to get things done, industrial countries face a choice. They can consume more energy and drive its price higher, making goods more expensive and causing inflation and declining wages; or they can make the economy more informative by developing methods of production and patterns of consumption that use less energy and capital resources and more knowledge. Inevitably, we have chosen and will choose the latter. It is this transition from a mass economy to an informative economy that is causing world economic crisis.

The crisis of the developed nations is concentrated at the top of the economy, not at the bottom. Historian Fernand Braudel divides the economy of capitalist nations into three distinct segments, the top one of which encompasses the large governing institutions of international banks, multinationals, and centralized political administration. Under this is the market economy, the making and selling of goods—businesses, stores, shops, and farms. Submerged further, but just as important, is what Braudel calls "material life," the constant and undefined activity of sharing and barter, the giving and taking and making of objects and services between people in local areas. This most basic level—a "rich zone, like a layer covering the earth"—and the market economy above it have changed dramatically in the past decade in response to higher prices for energy, higher costs for capital, and declining wages. We are changing our behavior, and as we do, the top of the economy, whose existence depends on its ability to control and manipulate the lower levels, is in crisis. Big businesses are threatened, banks face insolvency, and governments are rapidly turned over as successive economic failures destroy the confidence of voters. While governments and politicians debate their course of action, consumers, householders, and businessmen are already adapting.

Adaptation to the rising cost of energy is creating the informative economy. Industry is inventing more efficient manufacturing processes and redesigning products so that they use lighter, more durable materials and require smaller amounts of capital investment as well as less energy to produce. American cars weigh 30 percent less than they did a decade ago, last longer, and are more fuel-efficient. New housing is smaller, uses fewer building materials, and needs less heating and cooling. Consumers wanting to preserve their standard of living are choosing those products that conform to this adaptation while shunning those that ignore it. The result is less consumption of material and energy (mass).

One way to reduce consumption is through microelectronics. The industrial age mechanized manual labor; now semiconductors and microprocessors are bringing technology to the mind—analysis, communication, design, and decision-making. The microprocessor imparts to manufacturing processes, products, and services much of the power of the human nervous system. Automobile engineers have discarded the bulky carburetor for electronic fuel injection in order to reduce waste and increase efficiency. The Boeing 767, part of the new generation of fuel-efficient aircraft, could not have been designed without computers. Such repetitive service occupations as bank teller and telephone operator are being replaced by silicon-chip microprocessors. This is how information is replacing mass—by revolutionizing the design, creation, and function of goods and services. Whether in satellites or subcompact cars, toasters or tractors, semiconductor technology is reducing the size, cost, and energy requirements of products while making them more sophisticated, intelligent, and useful.

Whether the conservation of mass is accomplished through the new techniques of computer technology or the old virtues of workmanship and design, the informative economy comprises those individuals, companies, and institutions who understand that every unit of physical resource, regardless of whether it is a gallon of oil, a ton of steel, or a stand of timber, will need greatly increased intelligence (informed activity) to transform raw material into the components of truly economic goods or the instruments of effective services. The ratio between mass and information is changing and it must continue to change. Our prosperity depends on it.

This book is a description of the next economy and how to make the transition to it. Most economists look at the economy piecemeal and try to create a composite meaning. I propose to attempt to look at the whole of our economic life in order to understand our individual activity. It is not an attempt to tear down the walls of the industrial age, or to snipe at it with the advantage of hindsight. Rather, it is a look at what our reactions are to the tumultuous economic changes of the past decade. The book offers an alternative definition of intelligent economic behavior, not as a proposal but as an observation of present reality. It is clear that bearing up under economic difficulties are resourceful human beings adapting quickly to new circumstances, while above us, as always, to use John Maynard Keynes's famous epigram, are otherwise "practical men [who are] the slaves of some defunct economist."

❋ Chapter 1

The Decline of the Mass Economy

P art of the economy dies every day and is replaced by something new. This ceaseless activity of beginnings and endings, of new products and old habits, reflects how we change as a people, as a culture, and as a nation. During the past ten years, the economy has changed faster than at any previous time in our history, including the Great Depression, and has become so surprising, confusing, and unsettling that it is now the central concern in the lives of people and their government.

The overriding anxiety affecting daily economic life is the fear that our investments, livelihood, employer, or business could become a part of that which dies. Given this uncertainty, the economic decisions we make are difficult at best, risky at least. Should one buy a house, go back to school, change a job, move away, expand production? Knowing whether or not we are going into a recession is not enough. During the three recessions since 1974, some industries have failed while others have flourished. We need to know what will thrive and what will die—and why. Without that knowledge, the best education and effort are useless. More specifically, we need to know, within a field or industry, why some companies prosper and others stagnate.

The present economic tumult can best be understood when one considers the fact that two different, overlapping economies exist side by side in the United States: the economy of mass production and consumption of material goods, and a new, "informative" economy that reduces the amount of materials consumed by industry and individuals by raising and enhancing the intelligence and information contained within goods and services. In mature industrial societies such as our own, consumers are experiencing the decline of the mass economy and the rise of the informative economy. To understand how the informative economy is emerging, it is important to understand why the mass economy is declining, since the success of the first is a direct result of the structural changes and limits of the second.

The "mass" economy is the economy of the industrial age. Specifically, the mass economy occupied the period from 1880 until today, a time during which oil, the internal combustion engine, and the widespread generation and distribution of electrical power transformed nations into complex industrialized, consumer-oriented societies. The word *mass* is apt because the dominating economic force during this time was the substitution of fossil fuels for human energy in order to produce mass (physical goods) for the masses (consumers). Throughout this period, individuals, companies, and nations accumulated great amounts of goods, capital, and property. Inexpensive energy and cheap transportation enabled regional companies to become national companies, and their names became household words; industrial empires of enormous power and scale were assembled. Until 1973, up to which time the cost of energy fell while the consumption of energy rose, industrialized nations were able to amass great wealth.

The age of the mass economy was marked by expansion, mass production, the degradation of the environment, technological innovation, affluence, an ethic of consumption, high wages, the specialization and division of labor, the declining durability of goods, and the professionalization of services.

The mass economy is being replaced by an economy based on the changing ratio between the mass and information contained in goods and services. Mass means the energy, materials, and embodied resources required to produce a product or perform a service. While the mass economy was characterized by economies of scale, by many goods being produced and consumed by many people, the informative economy is characterized by people producing and consuming smaller numbers of goods that contain more information. What is this information? It is design, utility, craft, durability, and knowledge added to mass. It is the quality and intelligence that make a product more useful and functional, longer-lasting, easier to repair, lighter, stronger, and less consumptive of energy.

The decline of the mass economy was the result of one important shift: the changing relation in value among labor (people), capital (money), and resources (energy). This change far outweighs any economic theory of what is happening. It will have a far greater impact than inflation, high interest rates, taxes, underemployment and slow or zero economic growth because this changing relationship is both the *cause* and *cure* of these symptoms. The shift started in 1973, when energy and capital rose in value (or cost) while the value of a worker's time began to decline. We are experiencing the impact of this shift as economic contraction, which in turn is causing these effects:

High Capital Costs: The rising cost of capital means that money is more expensive to obtain, hold, and use. This can be reflected in either high interest rates or inflation, or both. In the 1970s we experienced high inflation, and so far in the 1980s we've had high interest rates. This trend will continue until the transition from the mass to the informative economy is completed. The high cost of capital has had dramatic effects on the housing and auto industries. It has increased the purchasing cost for the consumer without increasing industry's revenues. This has reduced overall demand, weakened industry, and prompted consumers to keep cars and houses longer.

getting smaller

The Liquidation of Large Corporations: Businesses that depend on mass markets, cheap transportation, and predictable consumers are losing out to smaller, more nimble companies. As the mass economy wanes, corporations with large amounts of debt will have to either sell off assets or pay out inordinate amounts of cash in interest charges. Many corporations are currently paying out more in interest than in dividends, and some are borrowing more money each year than they are generating in profits. When inflation is taken into account, many of the Fortune 500 companies are smaller now than they were ten years ago.

Contraction of Government: Another large institution that is shrinking is government, both state and local. Like those of large corporations, government revenues are diminishing, and the end of the expansion of the mass economy means that the future growth of governments, in terms of additional tax revenues, is severely limited. Governments face the dilemma of either increasing taxes, which would further choke economic recovery and therefore revenues, or not increasing taxes, which would result in a decline in revenues because of economic stagnation. For example, in 1982 the state of Michigan had to get a letter of credit from a consortium of Japanese banks in order to receive market interest rates on its notes. Without the guarantee, the state would not have been able to afford the loan because its credit rating had dropped below the level of what many financial institutions define as credit worthiness.

The End of Mass Markets: Mass markets existed as long as the economy expanded and consumer markets grew. With markets stagnant and individual incomes slowly declining, people are buying cautiously, demanding more from products—the demand for more information per unit of mass—and are no longer so responsive to advertisements and corporate blandishments. In the future, one size will no longer fit all, and in most cases markets will no longer be national.

Reintegration of Production and Distribution: The rising cost of energy has raised transportation and distribution costs. This will lead to more companies combining the manufacture of products with direct sales to the consumer. This will eliminate middlemen and complicated sales channels in order to deliver a higher-quality product at a competitive price. Such businesses include factory outlets, mail-order companies, and stores where foods are prepared on the premises. In addition, individuals, in order to save time, money, and travel, will create for themselves goods and services they formerly bought.

Shift in Sovereignty Over Capital: The eighties will be the decade of the saver. Those with cash to lend will do far better than those who borrow. A fifty-year trend during which borrowers made more money than savers has ended. Savers will take more control over their money as the high cost of capital rewards the sellers rather than the buyers of capital.

Demonetization of Values: "Everything has a price" will fade into "everything has value." As money becomes more fickle and unpredictable as a measure of value because of inflation/deflation, high tax rates, and volatile policy shifts in government, people and institutions will search for alternatives to cash. Already, 25 percent of world trade is done by barter, and the underground economy in the United States is estimated to be between 10 and 22 percent of the gross national product.

The single most important trend to understand is the changing ratio between mass and information in goods and services. This change will decide whether your present employer will be in business a decade from now. If you own a business, it will determine whether your company will grow or diminish. It will tell you whether your chosen study or career will be rewarded or ignored in the future. It will accurately predict the chances of success of products and services in the marketplace. It will tell you if your wages will go up or down in the coming years. And it will tell you where to invest, how to invest, and when to invest.

When I speak of the shift to an informative economy, understand that this means more than mere computerization. The age of electronic information is certainly upon us, and its effects will be multitudinous and powerful. But the word *informative* is used here to describe a broader scope of economic change. One dictionary defines *inform* as the capacity "to imbue or inspire something with a higher quality." The quickening and miniaturization of computational abilities is one important aspect of the shift from mass to informativeness, but it is not the shift itself.

The mass economy is synonymous with economies as a whole. Within economic science are deeply rooted assumptions about what healthy economic behavior is. Of these, the primary and least questioned is growth. An economy that does not grow is "ill" because it immediately produces undesired symptoms: unemployment, falling productivity, lowered real income, social unrest. A growing economy produces the material things we want: more goods, higher wages, more employment, and, from these, a sense of overall prosperity. During the past ten years, the ability of industrialized countries to achieve sustained growth has greatly weakened, and with that weakening have emerged both familiar and new problems, for which ready solutions are lacking. In the United States and in some areas of Europe, unemployment rates in 1982 were the highest since the Depression. The $5.2 trillion debt (personal, corporate, and governmental) in the United States threatens to forestall economic recovery. Purchase of a new home for many middle-class families is now nearly impossible. Formerly solid corporations teeter on the brink of bankruptcy.

The problems of slow economic growth are common to virtually every industrialized nation in the West, and while strategies differ, each shares identical goals: reducing inflation and unemployment while increasing production and real economic growth. These are laudable goals, but we may be looking at the wrong solutions. The maturation of the mass economy does not mean that the economy is sick, but, rather, that it is trying to change. The culmination of the mass economy is the beginning of a new economy, and our attempts to right the old economy are working against our own best interests. If we allow ourselves only one view of what an economy should be, we will be unable to see the opportunities that exist in the present situation. More important, if we cannot understand what the present is telling us, we will be oblivious to the real message it contains.

We are approaching an economic watershed. To a large extent, those who understand it will have the means to act intelligently; those who do not understand will find themselves the victims of this chaotic economy. We must realize that in the end, the economy is the interaction between us, the participants, and the earth, our environment. Therefore, the maturation and peaking of the mass economy means that we, and the world we live in, have changed irrevocably.

Before the eighteenth century, the great items of trade consisted largely of spices, tea, medicinal herbs, precious metals, and certain foodstuffs. Riches came from the land—from what it contained or could produce. Wealth was stored as gold. There were two ways to make a fortune: through taxation—a right of kings and feudal patriarchs—and through trade—buying goods cheaply in one place and selling them at a higher price in another. Though clothes were made, buildings built, and books bound, there was on the whole little process work done. Most of the population worked the land. Few went to school, and fewer still had hopes of independence and financial freedom. Most people lived on the level of subsistence.

How much of the world changed from an agrarian to an industrial economy is a story of invention and technology, synchronicity and genius, violence and greed, happenstance and discovery. But during the fifteenth century, before this change could occur, there already was in place throughout Europe an economy whose network consisted of roads to and from the Continent's nascent cities and towns. Though the town marketplace existed to exchange goods, most people did not "work" at a living; they made few distinctions among the many different activities that seem to rule our present-day lives. The ownership of land was fixed, save for war or inheritance. Production was labor-intensive. Money was saved but rarely lent, as interest was usury. Working for self-gain could bring expulsion from the church. Making an unseemly profit was seen as divisive social behavior. Labor was not a separate economic entity. If wages rose, people worked less. There was little sense of advancement in society and therefore no need to strive beyond what was expected of one.

Between the fifteenth and seventeenth centuries, the market for goods expanded throughout Europe. Clusters of feudalities became kingdoms, kingdoms became nations. Nations sent fleets to gather goods, while at home the merchant class developed. After the Protestant Reformation the successful businessman was no longer shunned. While the aristocracy remained aloof from the transactions of the burghers and merchants, the succeeding centuries saw its development as a wealthy class sophisticated about the world, and especially about money. Money assumed its role as a measure of values, land became property to be traded, and labor became a commodity.

In the early eighteenth century Thomas Newcomen perfected the steam engine to the point where it could be used to pump water from coal mines. Until then, the mines in England had quickly filled with water, limiting the amount of coal that could be extracted. By the late eighteenth century the steam engine was vastly improved in efficiency, and coal was readily available to power flour mills, textile factories, and rolling mills through the use of these new engines. Factories rose along waterways in the English Midlands, in Continental Europe, and in New England. The buildings were made of wood and brick and housed machinery driven by elaborate systems of pulleys, belts, and wooden gears that produced goods almost around the clock. Steam-powered machinery increased beyond previous imaginings the productivity of an uneducated labor force.

The impact of coal was that it centralized society. Except for heating and coking furnaces, coal's primary use was in driving large steam turbines that allowed factories and industrial plants to be situated away from conventional, water-driven sources of power. Coal-driven steam turbines later generated electricity that enabled the concentrated urban environment to work. In addition, coal-fired boilers could heat large buildings and skyscrapers while producing electricity to light streets and run elevators and trolleys.

Nevertheless, in 1850 fully 90 percent of the fuel energy used in the United States was still derived from wood, not coal. Rapid deforestation and expanding demand eventually made the price of coal more attractive, and in 1885 coal exceeded wood in energy usage. At this time, petroleum, discovered in this country in 1859 and used in the 1860s as a cheap substitute for whale oil in lamps, began to be found in greater quantities. By 1889, 100 million barrels of oil per year were being sold in the United States, two-thirds of it as kerosene for lamps and one-third as a cheap fuel to replace coal. By 1890, with the advent of the internal-combustion engine and the automobile, steam engines began to be phased out.

With the concurrent development of electricity, the dynamo, small electric motors, and agricultural mechanization at the end of the nineteenth century,

the mass economy was fully in place. A confluence of
forces created the wondrous inventions that seem so
mundane today: steel, central heating, boilers, engines,
telephones, skyscrapers, light bulbs, and phonographs.
The emphasis on manufacturing and production processes that were fuel-intensive meant that each person
would consume increasing amounts of energy. Between 1900 and 1910, manufacturing horsepower quintupled from 9.8 million to 48.5 million. By 1971, this
usage had increased to 21 billion horsepower. Petroleum consumption quadrupled in the first decade of
the century. Between the turn of the century and 1920,
the use of electric motors in manufacturing processes
increased twenty-seven times. Throughout this period,
oil was being discovered everywhere, and its price was
falling.

The rapid growth of energy-intensive industries increased the demand for energy, which reduced its price.
During the late nineteenth century, oil producers strove
to convert coal users to oil so that excess production
could be absorbed, the effect of which was to drive
the price of both coal and oil lower. As energy became
cheaper, the prices of iron, steel, and manufactured
products were lowered, which stimulated demand and
further increased the consumption of energy. Energy
prices dropped, lowering the prices of manufactured
products further. This intertwining and mutually reinforcing pattern of growth and energy development continued, except for periods of economic recession, for
nearly a hundred years, until 1973. The fact that this
ever-increasing cycle of demand and production was
self-feeding confused many into thinking that it was
also self-sustaining—a confusion that exists to this day.

While coal was a centralizing force, petroleum and
the internal-combustion engine had the opposite effect.
With the automobile, the city exploded its perimeter.
As their number increased, from 8,000 vehicles in 1900
to 27 million in 1930, automobiles created a vast ex-

pansion of formerly concentrated cities. Although central cities continued to grow, their suburbs grew faster. In 1947 central cities in the United States began losing population, reversing a 200-year-period of growth. It is no coincidence that 1947 was the year in which the consumption of gasoline first exceeded that of coal, reflecting in part the shift from urban to suburban living.

In the suburbs, families created in their homes aspects of both city and country. This meant an enormous duplication of goods that had been either shared in the city or used more productively on the farm. Backyards became miniparks with recreational, barbecue, horticultural, and zoological areas. After World War II, the American homeowner became, in social critic Philip Slater's words, an "Ace Hardware junkie." Each garage held hundreds of tools and implements that had earlier been wielded by the professional. The suburban householder became part plumber, electrician, painter, mechanic, car washer, gardener, landscaper, roofer, and handyman. Like so many cultures before us, we chose the rich as exemplars and built pseudo-estates with Doric columns, porticoes, atriums, swimming pools, and broad greenswards.

The mass economy created a consumer who burned increasing amounts of energy to support a life-style that was without precedent. Cheap energy enabled towns, neighborhoods, and families to consume vast amounts of resources and produce little in return. The mass economy assumed that each person would have more and more "stuff" as time went on.

With the question of supply seemingly solved by the magnificent endowment of our planet, economics focused almost exclusively on demand, employment, and the distribution of goods. While there were occasional doubts expressed about the fairness and social equitableness of the mass economy, few doubted its capacity to produce. In this sense it was neither capitalist nor socialist; the mass economy was not a system of economics but a structure that subsumed economics. And because there was little doubt that—given proper capital, industriousness, and resources—more and more goods could be produced, economics became on the whole a "science" to increase production and extend distribution. Economics was in essence mass economics. During the nineteenth and twentieth centuries, the questions raised by this untold wealth were hardly economic ones; rather, they were political. Even during the Great Depression, it was not for lack of material that the system collapsed. While migrants killed lizards for dinner on the road to California, milk and grain were dumped or burned. In the 1930s, oil became almost "worthless." Not until 1973, when it soared in value, did the world stop and wonder if indeed there were enough resources to support the mass economy.

The expansion of the mass economy was fueled, literally and figuratively, by this fundamental fact: during the past hundred years, labor has been replaced by fossil fuels. Through technology we replaced manual systems of production with industrialized, automated, fuel-driven production processes, and their efficiency guaranteed the growth of the economy. A U.S. citizen commands, in Btu equivalent, the services and goods of a hundred slaves. In other words, without fossil fuels, you would need a hundred menials to continue your current life-style. We take this ease for granted because we were born into it; it is the very fabric of our lives, and most of us do not want to see this condition change. It would mean less money, fewer goods, harder work for longer hours, less leisure time. We achieved this standard of living because the real cost of fossil fuels—our energy—went down between 1880 and 1973. Because of the relative abundance of oil, the more of it we used, the less it cost. As long as this seemingly inexhaustible and wonderful phenomenon continued, greater production and distribution of oil helped deliver more goods for less cost, and our wealth increased.

Naturally, such a supply of goods produced as its necessary corollary a consuming and, it might be added, a rather exploitative society. No matter how Puritan we may have been when we entered the era of mass production, the onslaught of goods wore away at the work ethic and eventually produced an accompanying ethic of consumption. We became, unwittingly perhaps, an exploitative society because at the heart of the mass economy is the wholesale extraction of fossil fuels, minerals, timber, and other resources. The dominant means of amassing wealth and power in the mass economy was the exploitation of natural resources, because it was in their transformation that the great profits of industry were to be found.

This exploitation affected, in ways both hidden and seen, our relationships with other peoples (in the form of colonialism and imperialism), our environment, our personal relationships, relationships between employers and employees, between men and women, between companies. The behavior was aggressive, competitive, and, in many cases, harsh.

Out of the mass economy grew intermediation. Intermediation is the insertion into an economic system of specialized goods and services that allows it to expand its scope, scale, and effect. Anyone who has created a small business or who has watched one become a medium to large business has seen that as the enterprise grows, the nature of the tasks and functions within the organization changes. At first, everyone does everything, from answering phones to carrying out the trash. But before long, one person sits at a switchboard and does nothing but answer the phone while another does nothing but empty the trash. Acts become "intermediated" within the organization. Instead of calling someone up, you have your switchboard operator do it. She waits until the WATS line is open. Instead of cleaning up your own space, the janitors do it at night. Instead of writing a note to a supplier, you dictate to someone in a steno pool. Because of expansion, simple tasks are done by others. Instead of doing something directly, persons in a large organization have intermediaries. Instead of sitting down with an owner of a building to negotiate a lease, you and the owner have lawyers—intermediaries—to do it for you. Why? Because growth produces differentiation and complexity. And complexity requires specialization. And when you are doing something specialized, someone else must do the things that you can no longer do because you are busy specializing.

The argument for intermediation is efficiency: it is more efficient to have a system where everyone is doing what they do best most of the time—this creates a productive factory or business. While this has been true, it does not follow that intermediary goods and services in themselves will always make a society more efficient and productive, which is a point that will be discussed in Chapter 8. Intermediation is the child of growth, and the mass economy was foremost an economy of expansion. As the economy expanded in all directions and as the various components within the economy developed, new intermediary goods, services, jobs, and technologies were demanded and created. Not only did industry require highly specialized intermediary goods and services: our lives did as well.

As an example, take the farm. From a largely self-sufficient economic unit that produced most of the food required for a family, where much of the energy was provided *in situ* through animals, and where even hand tools were at least repaired if not made, the farm has become but a single component in a vastly larger web of intermediary activities. A farmer's personal food is no longer grown on the farm. The farm may produce pigs, corn, or wheat, but the farmer's food is bought at stores to which it is trucked on roads requiring service stations, asphalt contractors, federal agencies, and motels for teamsters hired by corporations that lease Detroit-made rigs from banks who finance their loans by reselling certificates of deposit to pension funds or financial institutions. The banks require computers to monitor their complex activities as well as large office centers in cities to which their educated personnel can travel by day, only to return at night to homes scattered upon what was once rich, fertile soil—no longer farmland because it was more profitable for the farmer to sell land than food. To produce a crop to sell so that the farmer can buy food at the store, the farmer first buys hybrid seed grown in Costa Rica the previous winter and uses leased or purchased equipment requiring the same complex financial intermediation as a trucking company. He buys fertilizer produced by a large petroleum company that has piped natural gas across a desert through a $500 million pipeline into a tanker where it is first frozen, then shipped across an ocean, and finally manufactured into the fertilizer anhydrous ammonia.

For the process of growing the food we eat, which is a highly integrated activity of production, distribution, and consumption, we now have a system that requires the skills of many different persons, from graphic designers of packages to room-service maids, from roustabouts to waitresses, from chemical engineers to metallurgists. We have increased our production of foodstuffs many times, but we have also scattered and fractured our lives in a way that has left us with well-paid jobs but little economic control. Intermediation has brought us much of what we like about the mass economy, but it has required us to give up much of our lives to singular tasks.

While the mass economy was expanding and creating a seemingly endless array of new livelihoods and products, its underlying goal was to eliminate labor. One of the great contradictions of the mass economy is that it succeeds only insofar as it makes labor unnecessary, since its productivity is measured only by the ratio of labor to output. When more goods are produced by equal or lesser amounts of labor, the economy has increased its productivity. If a hundred people working together for one day produce 100 radios and if the next day they produce 103 radios, their productivity is said to have increased 3 percent. Because of the substitution of fuel-driven technologies for human labor, the mass economy produced more goods more cheaply. As productivity increased, wages went up, prices came down, and the demand for goods increased. With increased demand, new factories were built, employing even more people, and this spiral of growth became self-feeding. Because newer factories were even more productive, employing the latest labor-saving techniques, our ability to produce more caused an ever-rising spiral of production, employment, consumption, demand, higher wages and production. Higher production was accomplished not by people working ever more furiously but by people "working" less while machines worked more. Which brings us to the fundamental reason energy is so valuable: through machinery, it does the work that humans did. Electricity, natural gas, coal, and gasoline—all accomplish work formerly done by people. To increase our output in the mass economy, we hired machines and fossil fuels instead of people. Fuels were far cheaper and more reliable. For not only was energy decidedly inexpensive, but, until 1973, its cost was falling. When oil was cartelized and the price rose 500 percent, it was as if our hundred Btu servants went out on strike and came back twenty-four hours later with a new contract. This so-called OPEC tax on production was not merely a tax—it was as dramatic a shift in structure as the emergence of the labor movement was in the early decades of this century.

While the mass economy was steadily making labor less necessary, employment nevertheless increased dramatically because much of the labor force was involved with all aspects of economic expansion. Housing, construction, highways, utilities, research, government, hotels, automobiles, energy, chemicals, trucking, paper, clothing, appliances, plastics, and machine tools—to name only a few—were all industries that expanded in order to supply and service new economic growth. And in turn their expansion created further demand and growth. Thus the mass economy could have nearly full employment while concentrating on creating production methods involving technologies that used fewer and fewer people. It was a formula that seemed unstoppable. The United States became a great power, the Western industrial nations seemed like winners, and the world experienced in the thirty years after World War II an almost convulsive surge of material prosperity.

The basic strength of the mass economy is also its weakness—the increase of productivity through the substitution of fuel. For when the mass economy stops growing or when its rate of growth slows considerably, large numbers of people whose basic job is to provide the goods and services required for further expansion are thrown out of work. And as happened in the Depression, if the economy cannot recover and begin to grow again, then the momentum of continually increasing production, demand, wages, and jobs reverses into falling demand, falling employment, and falling wages. The mass economy, to function at its best, must grow robustly.

Robust growth was achieved by robust use of energy. Technology transformed energy into labor-saving productivity, but this emphasis on production techniques caused a curious anomaly. As more goods were produced, they became on the whole less durable and thus less valuable. If our radio factory of a hundred workers produced 103, 150, or 200 radios per day, it was said to have increased its productivity 3, 50, or 100 percent, respectively. But this increase in productivity did not mean that the radios were as good as the radios produced when the factory produced 100 per day. In fact, increased productivity may have meant that the new radios wouldn't last nearly as long as the old ones. ·

As the mass economy achieved its greatest growth in the fifties and sixties, critics such as Vance Packard damned the tendency of U.S. manufacturers to make products into which obsolescence was designed. The "wastemakers" certainly did that, but there were some basic reasons why this could have occurred. After all, if in earlier times a manufacturer had created an obviously poor product, one that the buyer could easily realize would not last, it would not have been bought and thus not produced. But that was not the case after World War II. As both manufacturers and consumers, we participated in an orgy of excess that will never be rivaled again. In a way, it was more "economic" to buy cheaper goods and replace them later than it was to buy a more expensive product at the outset. How could this be, since it contradicts common sense and economic dogma?

The period between 1950 and 1973 has been referred to as the "golden age of industrialism." Historically it was the longest sustained period of prosperity and, more important, of advances in worker productivity. With productivity consistently rising 3 to 4 percent every year, wages rose rapidly while prices went down in relation to the buying power of those wages; in effect, goods became cheaper every year. Underlying this phenomenon, and critically important to it, was the fact that every year fossil fuels were becoming less expensive. The world seemed awash in energy, so much so that in 1959 President Eisenhower placed restrictions on imported oil to protect domestic oil companies. With cheaper energy going into more efficient means of production, America had its halcyon days. And what did it do? It overate. Never in the history of the world was there a period where so many became so affluent so quickly as after World War II. As prices of goods fell in relation to wages, a curious phenomenon resulted. Since goods were getting cheaper all the time (as well as changing, at least superficially, every year), there was no longer any perceived benefit in purchasing those goods that would last the longest but were also more expensive. With affluence spreading, the natural tendency was to buy goods that were mediocre or just acceptable in quality for the sake of being able to buy a larger variety of goods. Manufacturing, advertising, and marketing became enchanted with this new consumer: the solidly middle-class blue- or white-collar worker who for the first time in history consistently had more money to spend on discretionary purchases than the year before. If consumers could get a washing machine for $200 instead of $300, they could spend the other $100 on a toaster, a rotisserie, and an electric can opener. And, anyway, if the less expensive washer lasted only five years, so what? In five years a new washer might still sell for $200 while wages would have continued to rise, making the washer cheaper still.

Because production, retailing, advertising, and distribution had all become gigantic in scale to meet this demand for goods, smaller manufacturers were crowded out and bad products drove out good ones. I had a friend who produced some of the finest olives in the San Joaquin Valley of California. He got his big break when a large food chain began buying small amounts of his canned olives. As time went on and the volume of his sales increased, the chain not unreasonably asked for volume discounts. Production increased further, money poured in, and the olive producer borrowed money to increase his output. Again the chain increased its order, but again it asked for further price discounts. Again he complied, but in order to do so he took production shortcuts that affected the quality of his olives. A year later, he received a larger order requiring further price discounts. By this time, my friend was not making money and barely hanging on. His only hope was that the chain would increase its order the following year so that he could get back into the black. The chain did, but it also asked him to lower his price again. This time, he had to make a choice: lower his quality and break even or maintain his quality and lose money. He chose the latter, lost money for a year, and then went out of business when the purchasing contract was not renewed the following year.

This story was repeated thousands of times in other endeavors and businesses in the United States. It is a sorry tale for the producer who lost his business, but it is just as sorry for the consumer who in the end got stuck with a decidedly inferior olive. Once U.S. manufacturers realized the gains to be made by increasing scale and cutting costs, the mass economy became an unstoppable force: large, powerful, efficient, and decidedly mediocre. Because of this, many American companies lulled themselves into poor competitive positions internationally. Now that people are thinking twice before they buy, U.S. products don't look so good to us either. Many of us buy foreign instead, which means a loss of jobs.

The mass economy has peaked because cheap energy, the underlying driving force, is gone. Productivity is falling because rising productivity depended almost solely on our ability to gain access to inexpensive energy. Energy costs have soared because the demand for fuel by a continually growing mass economy finally confronted the inherent limitations of the earth to supply that energy cheaply. And people, seeing that the future may not bring higher wages and lower-priced goods, are buying the products that save them from having to rebuy later at a higher price. Much of the business community in the United States, having misread the future, took the wrong road. The future of America now belongs to individuals and companies, large and small, that understand the shift in emphasis from mass to information and can meet it.

This means that many jobs will be lost in the old industries of the mass economy, and particularly in those companies that have not adapted during the last decade to the new relationship among labor, capital, and energy. Professor M. Harvey Brenner of Johns Hopkins University recently told a House subcommittee that "The most important difference between this recession and most others is that it reflects structural change in the economy. Many workers in the extractive and manufacturing sectors are not going to find reemployment at their old jobs, nor are their sons and daughters or younger brothers and sisters going to find work careers in these . . . industries." In other words, the very industries that provided the mass economy with its impetus and muscle—steel, automobiles, and durable goods—are contracting.

Chapter 2

The Rise of Oil

For the first seventy years of this century, the mass economy saw wages rise, the cost of capital remain steady, and the price of energy fall. What has happened, as shown in Table 1, is that in 1973 energy costs reversed their historical descent and began to climb. This is not news, but it raises this question: Is this rise temporary or long-term? Is it a mere aberration or a fundamental economic shift? There has been debate over the meaning of oil price rises since 1973, but in the economy it is the actual market price, not interpretations of the market, that determines how the economy functions. The oil markets are saying that the long fall in energy prices has ceased and has now begun a rising pattern. The arguments that shifting to coal and nuclear energy will reduce oil consumption, that solar and other forms of renewable energy are the answer,

Table 1*

Time	World Price of Oil† (1967 constant dollars)	U.S. Price (constant dollars)
1870	$ 9.82	$ 9.82
1880	4.53	4.53
1890	2.66	2.66
1900	3.80	3.80
1910	2.55	2.55
1920	4.42	4.42
1930	2.62	2.62
1940	2.59	2.59
1950	3.23	3.23
1960	3.45	3.45
1970	1.79	2.46
1973 (pre-OPEC)	1.95	2.77
1974	7.92	4.43
1975	7.14	4.51
1976	6.77	4.56
1977	6.85	4.49
1978	6.51	4.43
1979	7.82	4.97
1980	12.75	12.75
1981	12.47	12.47

* Table adapted from *Oil and Gas Journal*; *World Oil*; Historical Statistics of the United States M 76-92; Statistical Abstract No. 1034, 1980; Statistical Abstract No. 859, 1950; Statistical Abstract No. 974, 1960.

† The fall and rise of prices did not occur in a straight progression. After both wars, oil prices rose, and there was concern about shortages. Some economic analysts have contended that the price of oil has been highly politicized and therefore does not reflect the true market value. This argument is something of a red herring, and my purpose in showing the prices of oil since its discovery is that they reveal the overall pattern or movement of the market apart from the short-term machinations that have always surrounded oil. To illustrate this, the right-hand column, showing U.S. oil prices, reflects the government's efforts after 1970 to control prices and mitigate the effect the world market prices for oil would have had on the economy. Just as the Standard Oil Trust manipulated oil prices for its own ends in the late nineteenth century, the U.S. government tried the same. In the end, the market dominates.

and that OPEC will be broken and the price of oil will fall will remain just that—arguments.

For all of us, the questions can be reduced to one: Is the cost of energy in relation to the cost of capital and labor going up or down? Believing that energy costs will go down over the coming decades will point us to one set of actions; believing that they will continue to rise will point to a different set. The government's economic policy is based on the former assumption—that the cost of energy will resume a downward trend and that the long historical relationships among labor, capital, and energy can be reestablished, producing growth and increased production. I believe in the latter assumption as will be explained in this chapter.

As early as 1950 came predictions of oil shortages within ten to twenty years. In 1962, M. King Hubbert, a research physicist for the U.S. Geological Survey, delivered his now classic *Energy Resources* report to the National Academy of Sciences, in which he said U.S. oil production would peak between 1966 and 1971. In 1970 it rose to 3.5 billion barrels a year and has been falling since. Hubbert's warning of oil shortages was ignored until OPEC demonstrated the implications of those shortages simply and forcefully.

A cartel depends on a single assumption—that it can control enough of a resource to ensure a quasi-monopoly. For almost a decade, until the "oil glut" of 1982, that assumption stood unchallenged. There currently may be an overproduction of oil, but the oil that is most critical to the world lies in the Middle East; this pool of oil is of great importance because it is the largest amount available to other countries. The United States, the Soviet Union, and China have large oil reserves, but little of it is available to others, with the exception of the Soviet Union's oil, which supplies Communist Europe. For the United States, Asia,

Western Europe, and the world's developing nations, the most important oil lies adjacent to the Persian Gulf.

What happened in 1973–74 was not the result of the sudden avarice of a few Arab nations. The price rises confirmed the fact that the West's demand for oil at that time was soaring above production capacity. In a mere twenty-year period, between 1950 and 1970, the United States changed from being the largest producer of oil to the largest importer. Between 1962 and 1972, Europe's demand for oil increased by 170 percent, Japan's by 380 percent, and the United States' by 60 percent. (Because we were already the world's largest user, our growth was smaller in percentage terms.) In those ten years the total demand for oil among Western nations increased by nearly 19 million barrels a day, an amount that exceeds present OPEC production.

The Yom Kippur War between the Arabs and Israelis politicized oil, and the hostilities became the justification for embargoes, production cuts, and price rises aimed at Western nations that supported Israel. But the war was not the underlying cause of oil's rise in price; the principal cause was simply demand. Before the war began in October 1973, oil prices had been rising sharply in world markets. When the OPEC oil ministers met in Iran just before Christmas 1973, they raised the price of their oil to $11.65 a barrel from a posted price of $2.59 a year earlier. This fundamentally altered the world economy of the previous ninety years because it changed the relationship between labor and energy—the structural foundation of the mass economy.

The 1973 oil embargo and the subsequent rise in prices focused global attention on the problem of the depletion of resources. Commencing with the Club of Rome report in 1972, which predicted shortages of critical raw materials by the beginning of the next century, the world became concerned about whether there were enough physical resources in the earth to sustain developed economies. That we will run out of critical resources sooner or later is not an issue I want to argue, and it is not the most helpful way of looking at an economy. It is far more revealing to look at the change in the relative value of energy compared with labor and capital since it is the relationship among these three that determines the structure of our economy.

Because the mass economy is fundamentally a transfer of fossil-fuel energy to production through technology mediated by human labor, any change in one of the components will affect the overall economy. Technology can become more sophisticated and productive; labor can produce more through better technology; energy can be substituted for labor; or labor can be substituted for energy. Any changes in these will have an effect on the price of goods, the value of labor, the amount of goods produced per unit of labor, and the amount of energy used in their production. But whereas the price of labor and goods is a result of the relationship between them and the cost of energy, the cost of fossil fuels is determined by more unyielding principles. Oil is limited in total supply, nonrenewable, and available only in certain places, and labor and capital are required to extract it. Theoretically, if an economy became totally labor-intensive, the demand for nonhuman energy would be nonexistent and the value of that energy would be zero. But we are in the latter stages of a mass economy that is absolutely dependent on the consumption of extraordinary amounts of nonhuman energy in order to sustain its growth and health. To give an example of this extraordinary dependency, it was announced on November 16, 1982, that the largest oil deposit discovered since the 1968 Prudhoe Bay strike in Alaska was found near Point Arguello off the California coast. This find, estimated by industry observers to contain 1 billion barrels of recoverable oil, will take twenty years to develop but, in total, will provide the United States with a two-month supply of oil.

We have depended on the growth of the mass economy for rising wages and income. Our wages can go up only if the prices of goods go down in relation to those wages, and this can only happen if we produce more. As our human physical limits are well known, the means by which we produce more is through technology and machinery. In this and many other ways, the mass economy has been hugely successful. From 1948 until 1966, productivity in the United States increased by slightly more than 3 percent a year, the longest and largest sustained measured rate of growth in history. If compounded, this rate of growth would increase our standard of living by a factor of twenty in a century, by four hundred in two centuries. From these figures alone we can see how difficult it would be to continue to achieve this increase in productivity. Imagine, if you can, a life four hundred times as abundant in goods and services two hundred years from now. It isn't conceivable, but our government's stated economic goals aim for a growth rate of 4 to 5 percent per year. Because the primary way to increase productivity is through energy and technology, productivity gains must be accomplished through better machines working faster and harder in transforming more matter into finished products. When people ask, "What's the matter with the economy?" the answer is *matter*—namely, oil. This matter is what fuels and creates the production of goods. A more prosperous mass economy could occur as long as the price of energy was fixed, went down, or rose more slowly than the overall increase in the rate of productivity. Between 1948 and 1966, worker productivity, taking inflation into account, rose 53 percent while the price of oil, adjusted for inflation, *fell* 56 percent. From 1973 through 1979, oil prices increased 300 percent (adjusted for inflation), while productivity for the entire period increased by a mere 2.5 percent. In 1980 oil doubled in price after the cutoff of Iranian oil, and productivity dropped 3.2 percent in one year, erasing the previous seven years' gain. Since then productivity has fallen further, unemployment has worsened, major areas of our industry have slumped to postwar lows, and the United States has entered its third sharp recession in eight years.

Now that we have the wisdom of hindsight in evaluating the unfolding of the mass economy, particularly the wealth gained through our ability to transform raw energy into productive capacity, it is fitting that we ponder the possible advantages and disadvantages of this new characteristic of energy—that is, that the more it is consumed, especially oil, the faster it rises in price. This is in marked contrast to the period between 1870 and 1970, during which oil became cheaper as more of it was used.

At present there seem to be three basic ways of looking at the future. The first is that we are entering an age of limits and that industrial nations must radically cut back their consumptive behavior if others are to have adequate resources. A second view is that the 1970s were atypical and that a combination of nuclear, fusion, oilshale, and solar energy projects will return to us our historical economic growth. The third is that the reduced production of energy is creating an opportunity in which society can transform itself by using less, sharing more, and becoming wiser. The first and third views are almost always rejected by government and the business community, the first because it says the game is over, the third because it is ideological and requires a fundamental change in our system of values, something that is simply unacceptable to the business community. (Why this is so is a mystery, since it is the business community, through its various marketing mechanisms, that assiduously studies value changes in our culture and then tries to exploit them through new products.) Thus government and business are left with the second view, which locks us into depending on increases in the amount of available energy. Can this happen?

Julian Simon, professor of economics at the University of Illinois, put forth the thesis in his book *The Ultimate Resource* that resources are becoming less scarce. Since Simon's book was widely praised by business publications and articulates the views of many conservative leaders, it is worthwhile to examine his way of thinking. Simon uses copper as his main example. Like many minerals, copper has fallen in price since the 1800s because of the increasing efficiency of its extraction, more intelligent prospecting, and better technology. But just as important, the demand for copper has dropped during the past few decades because of the growth of electronics, satellite communication, fiber optics, and microwave transmission. Because of copper's expense, more efficient substitutes were devised. Here it is important to distinguish between copper, a material, and oil, an energy resource. Copper only consumes energy—it does not produce it. Whether a phone call goes through an underground cable or a satellite, we will use energy, but not necessarily copper. While industrial society can substitute, rearrange, and eliminate the need for certain materials, it requires energy to do so. When we speak of raw materials, it is energy that is critical to our future, not the price of copper. The only table portraying oil prices that Mr. Simon uses appears in the appendix of his book, and it shows that between 1970 and 1979 the price of oil in constant dollars rose five times. Simon also illustrates in the same table how the rises in oil prices cause increased oil-well drilling, an act that might alleviate shortages. What Simon does not mention is that the increased drilling since 1973 has not increased our reserves, while the amount of energy and money required to drill a well is climbing. The price for "new" oil is now estimated at $8 to $10 per barrel, up from just over $1 a decade ago.

Hubbert pointed out in 1962 that it is wrong to assume increased oil exploration will increase reserves. The "finding rates" of oil have declined sharply since the 1930s while the expense per foot drilled has continued to climb. Hubbert recorded the highest finding rate in the early 1930s as 276 barrels per foot of exploratory drilling in the shallow fields of Texas and Oklahoma. By 1965 the finding rate had dropped to 35 barrels per foot and by the late 1970s to only 10 to 15 barrels of oil for every foot. A recent study by two Cornell University scientists, Charles Hall and Cutler J. Cleveland, points to a secondary and potentially more serious problem. The energy costs of exploring, developing, pumping, and distributing oil have gone up over the past forty years to the point that it now requires 1.5 barrels of oil to drill one foot. Taking the higher 1970s figure of 15 barrels as a finding rate, it now requires 10 percent of the energy recovered to discover and exploit the new energy. Hall and Cleveland say that as finding rates continue to drop and as energy exploration costs continue to rise, within twenty years the amount of energy removed in oil may be less than the amount of energy used to extract it.

Simon and others contend that since the cost of production of Persian Gulf oil is barely 40 cents per barrel, the market price for oil is highly inflated and therefore unsustainable. One could just as easily say that the original price of Manhattan was $24 in beads, and therefore it does not have worth greater than its cost. What determines market price is demand. Although Saudi oil is extremely cheap to find and produce, oil that can be found to compete with it is considerably more costly to produce and is becoming more so every year.

The reason for this is simple. While there are certain geological deposits of oil that are vast and relatively easy to tap (such as the deposits surrounding the Persian Gulf), they have already been found and are being exploited. I have a farm near a town called Petrolia, so named because early settlers noticed that oil was oozing out of the ground, which was a phenomenon that had been noticed in deserts surrounding the Persian Gulf for over a thousand years. After the "discovery" of oil in the United States in 1859, the fields first exploited were areas such as my local town, where oil was observably present and therefore easy to locate. Later, as geological and production techniques became more sophisticated, the areas of oil production were concentrated in places like Oklahoma and Texas, where oil was of high quality and cheap to obtain by a process similar to drilling for water. Between the late 1930s and the late 1960s, most of the great oil fields of the world were discovered, and oil production increased faster than the world's ability to consume it. Prices hit their historic lows during a time when the world was becoming increasingly proficient at consuming the abundant flow of energy: plastics, automobiles, synthetic textiles, agricultural fertilizers, and air travel converged with conventional usage to make petroleum the dominant source of world energy.

In the meantime, new deposits of oil were found, usually a little deeper in the ground, more remote, or not even on land but offshore. Some of the oil, such as shale oil and the heavy crudes, was not economical to extract or refine and was left in the ground. Exploration and development costs went up as oil was found in areas like the North Sea or the north slope of Alaska. Just as M. King Hubbert had predicted in 1962, the growth of the world's oil reserves and the oil industry began to approximate a rough bell curve, where production started out flat, grew slowly through the late nineteenth century, and then began an exponential rise, only to begin peaking in the late twentieth century. Moreover, since oil is finite in quantity (even if there is no agreement as to what that quantity is), a point is reached where the cost of oil production rises while the amount of oil produced remains constant. This is the opposite of the theory of mass production, which says that the more you produce, the cheaper a product will become—cars, for example. Because oil did become cheaper during the first hundred years of its use, its ultimate finite nature was often ignored. And because oil was produced at only a few cents per barrel in the early part of this century, the slow rise in its cost was hardly noticeable at first. After all, as oil production costs went from 5 cents to 25 cents a barrel, it was thought of not as a 400 percent increase but as a 20-cent increase. A similar rise from 25 cents to $1.25 was still acceptable. But now that a barrel of new oil costs $8 to $10 to find, increases in production costs have serious implications for the overall economy.

To understand why oil costs will go up faster than production, take as an example the California redwood, a tree considered highly desirable both for its beauty and its resistance to moisture and infestation. The redwood groves of northern California were thick and old, and trees grew to 300 feet in height and 30 feet in circumference. An explosion of industry occurred in the nineteenth century in the redwood forests as the biggest and most accessible stands were harvested and milled. San Francisco Bay was so thick with lumber schooners in 1870 that one could practically walk to Alcatraz island in the middle of the bay on the decks of the ships. Starting with more than 2 million acres, the lumber industry has managed to reduce the number of acres of virgin redwood to 80,000; needless to say, the price of redwood has soared. Because redwood is so slow to grow, the great stands are now gone. San Francisco was built of clear, select redwood, but it costs over $2,000 for a thousand board feet today, two hundred times as much as it did one hundred years ago.

Similarly, as the world draws off the oil from the easily established oil fields, it must replace this production with new fields. The president of Shell Oil, USA, John Bookout, contends that there is "as much oil to be discovered in this country as has been produced in our entire history." I do not doubt this. That is an exact description of the top of a bell curve. The first oil well was drilled 69.5 feet into the earth. Now oil will be found deep, sometimes 4 to 5 miles down. Instead of $50,000, the new deep probes can cost $20 million per well. There are now seagoing oil platforms that cost over $1 billion to construct. Newer land rigs are 13 stories high and can drill 9 miles into the earth. Exploration techniques now employ satellites, computers, and robotics. These new technologies will result in significantly higher development costs. There is no question that we will have oil throughout this century and the next, but there is also no question that this oil will be increasingly expensive. There is little chance of running out of oil, but there is a possibility of being *priced* out of oil.

Between 1972 and 1974, the American energy industry used 15 percent of all available U.S. capital in order to increase the development of energy in this country. Since that time, that figure has increased to 25 percent. What will it be in 1990, or 2020, as capital becomes an increasingly bigger component of the cost of energy? If we spend most of our available capital in order to create an economy that generates sufficient capital to create sufficient energy, we will find ourselves in a cycle that is self-defeating and ultimately unsustainable. Energy demand will make capital more expensive, until we will be unable to afford either capital or energy. Furthermore, we as a nation are not alone; the supply of energy must be shared with other countries.

Oil currently provides one-half of all energy consumed—more than double the amount used twenty years ago. While the rise in prices has caused oil demand to fall in industrial nations (U.S. consumption has dropped 17 percent since 1978), this does not necessarily mean that the overall world demand for oil will be reduced. In Western industrialized countries and Japan, the oil intensity (the proportion of oil in overall energy consumption) is falling as industry and consumers convert to coal and other energy sources and invest in energy conservation equipment. Furthermore, the historical linkage between economic development and energy growth no longer holds. Since 1977 the amount of energy required to produce a unit of GNP in the United States, Japan, and Europe has been declining. And many think that this decline can be extended much further, as there still clings to Western economies a margin of energy fat—that is, consumption of energy that is not productive but is, instead, reflective of waste and inefficiency.

But where Western nations can cut back, less-developed nations cannot. Most of the world is not yet industrialized but is rapidly moving toward development. Moving most slowly, but constituting the largest segment of the world's population, are the agrarian nations. Their 2.5 billion people currently consume the equivalent of approximately 5 billion barrels of oil a year. These countries, whose people live on a subsistence level, strive to make at least marginal improvements in their standard of living, but have no fat. It is estimated that by the end of this century their populations will number 3.5 billion and their energy consumption will nearly double, to the equivalent of 9 or 10 billion barrels a year. For developing agrarian countries, oil offers advantages that no other fuel possesses. These countries do not and probably will not have extensive electrical grids through which hydroelectric and coal-generated electricity can be channeled. Oil is easily divisible and transported without great hazard, and it can be used to power small tractors and equipment. As these countries urbanize, they require transport in the form of buses, taxis, and private automobiles. Diesel fuel for power generation can be transported to remote places where wood and natural gas cannot. These qualities of oil mean that lesser-developed countries will have far more difficulty in converting to alternative sources of energy than we will, and it is these countries that will increasingly demand oil over the coming decades.

Similarly, there are 600 million people living in nations on the threshold of industrial development who now consume the equivalent of 4.8 billion barrels of oil a year. By century's end, their number is expected to increase to 1 billion, and they will have to increase their energy consumption to approximately 15 billion barrels if they are to industrialize successfully. Nations that have industrialized since World War II, such as Taiwan, Korea, and Brazil, now account for another 600 million people and consume the energy equivalent of 15 billion barrels annually. Their rapid economic growth, if continued at reasonable rates, will increase their yearly energy consumption to the equivalent of 24 billion barrels. For these three groups of countries— agrarian, newly industrialized, and industrialized—energy consumption in oil equivalents will increase from a total of 25 billion barrels today to nearly 50 billion a year by the year 2000.

Even expensive energy can make the labor of these countries more productive, and this will increase their standard of living. But in postindustrial nations, where labor has already achieved extraordinary productivity and buying power, higher energy costs are causing economic dislocation and real drops in wages. So while we can reasonably expect postindustrial nations to use less energy over the next two decades because of energy efficiency gained in housing, automobiles, and industry—not only reducing the oil intensity of their economies but also severing the link between GNP growth and energy—this will have little effect on the increased demand for oil elsewhere.

However energy is allocated, as time goes on the amount of oil available for consumption will slowly

Table 2*

Year	World Population (billions)	World Oil Consumption (million barrels)	World Per Capita Consumption (barrels)
1890	1.55	149	.1
1910	1.70	327	.2
1920	1.81	688	.4
1930	2.02	1,412	.7
1940	2.25	2,144	.95
1950	2.53	3,803	1.50
1960	3.06	7,674	2.51
1965	3.34	11,058	3.31
1970	3.73	16,711	4.48
1973	3.96	20,368	5.15
1976	4.18	21,192	5.06
1978	4.33	21,192	5.04
1980	4.48	21,813	4.88
1981	4.56	20,404	4.48
(projected)			
1990	5.27	20,000	3.79
2000	6.19	20,000	3.23

* Table adapted from Statistical Abstract No. 1032, 1980; *International Petroleum Encyclopedia*, vol. 14, Tulsa: Penn Well Publishing Co., 1981; *World Population*, A. M. Carr-Saunders, 1925; *Atlas of World Population*, 1981; Statistical Abstract No. 1570, 1980; author's projections.

dwindle. As Table 2 reveals, our world per capita consumption of oil has risen dramatically throughout this century and has recently peaked. If we maintain the current levels of worldwide oil consumption of 20 billion barrels per year, per capita consumption of oil will drop by one-third by the end of the century. Although energy consumption has declined recently in postindustrialized nations, it is difficult to imagine the whole world willingly reducing its per capita consumption by one-third without demand exerting unusual pressure on prices and production.

Historically, the use of inexpensive energy guaranteed economic security for an industrialized nation. Postindustrialized nations, however, face a decade in which their reliance on energy may only impoverish them. This scenario of the world's energy use produces a curious fact: a barrel of oil is more valuable to a poor person than to a rich person. A gallon of gas in a small tractor in Mexico, Thailand, or Kenya is worth more than a gallon in a Chevrolet used to pick up some groceries at the store. In the first case, there is a productive increase; in the second, an increase in consumption. A person who uses a gallon of gas to till a plot for potatoes or corn is engaged in an act that will increase income. A person who drives to the store to pick up some ice cream and cigarettes is reducing his income. As the price of gasoline and consequently the cost of driving an automobile continues to rise, people will drive less if it is a consumptive act. If gasoline should hit $5 per gallon, we may well want to walk to the store, because we will save money, but the peasant will still buy the gallon of gas because when all is said and done, he will make money. Most of the world is grappling with economic *needs*; most people in industrialized nations are grappling with economic *wants*.

For the time being, the worker who drives the Chevrolet can outbid the peasant for a gallon of oil. But before long the peasant will outbid the middle classes. The developing nations can forgo almost everything except energy—particularly oil. Increased oil consumption is their key to increased income and security, while increased consumption for Western nations will only weaken their economies.

Thus oil will have a great equalizing effect. During the past decade Western nations have reached deeply into their capital reserves in order to purchase the energy required to maintain their standard of living. I believe that the reason we did not see a depression in 1974 similar to the one in 1929 was because of the enormous capital reserves built up in the United States since World War II. Those reserves, in the form of savings and investments, have been depleted since 1973 as the United States has had to pay additional tens of billions of dollars per year to the oil-producing countries. In place of this capital we have been substituting debt. The peaking of the mass economy because of its dependency on inexpensive energy for growth has created both this loss of capital reserves and a continually growing national debt. This debt is the underlying cause of the rise in cost of capital.

❋ Chapter 3

Debt and
Capital

The high cost of capital has had as great an effect on our daily lives as has the rise in energy prices. The "high cost of capital" refers here to inflation and high interest rates. If you are in business, an investor, or are trying to save, it is essential to know if the cost of capital will remain high and whether it will take the form of high interest rates, inflation, or both. This will determine whether your investments result in losses or gains, whether your business thrives or shrivels, or whether your savings grow or erode.

Economists define capital as the wealth available to invest in the production of new goods. In this sense, capital represents the surplus of production over consumption. For example, a farmer produces 200 tons of potatoes and sells them for $75 per ton, for a total of $15,000. This is his production. To run his tractor, buy his seed, rent the land, pick the crop, and pay his wages costs him $14,000. This is his consumption. The extra $1,000 becomes in effect new capital. He can invest it in new equipment, he can buy stock in another company, he can keep it in reserve in the bank, or he can go out on the town. If he buys a new piece of equipment, the equipment is the capital. If he buys a new storage bin, that is capital. Any investment he makes that will help him or others *produce* more can be said to be a capital investment. But if he spends the $1,000 on wine and song, it is not capital. It is consumption.

All economic systems, regardless of ideology, need capital investment to grow. In an undeveloped economy, people can be capital and are used as such when tools and equipment are not available. This is how China set about building up its country after World War II under Mao Zedong. The capital in more modern economies is transferred and invested in the form of money, and in this book, *capital* is used to mean the monetary wealth available for investment in the production of new wealth. In order for an economy to expand, capital must be made available and it must be invested in future production. Without this constant plowing back, economies falter. Just as important, if capital is invested in the wrong method of production— an unnecessary factory, a faulty invention, or the overproduction of goods—an economy can suffer because capital has been misallocated and produces no benefits.

Then what is the *cost* of capital? If it is derived from the surplus of production over consumption, why does it have a "cost" at all? To understand capital's cost, we have to understand the relationship between capital and money.

When the farmer sold his potatoes, he received money. When we think of money, we think of it as something that purchases. Money buys groceries or pays the cost of goods and services required to run a farm or build a factory. Money, then, is a commonly accepted medium of exchange that can be used as a measure of value. It is a means to buy and sell goods and services. It is something that can be *saved*. In the United States, money consists of all the coins and currency in circulation, plus demand deposits such as checking accounts. This is considered our "active" money supply and is referred to as the M1. If we add to this certificates of deposit, savings accounts, money-market accounts, and time deposits, we have a larger measure called the M2.

When the farmer sold his potatoes and was left with an extra $1,000, he decided that instead of buying new equipment, he would put the money in the bank and earn interest. In other words, the farmer "lent" the money to the bank for a period of time, for which the bank was willing to pay a fee. The bank, in turn, loaned the money to another farmer, who was willing to pay an even higher rate of interest. In other words, money earns money—which is to say, the use of money is bought and sold. In times when inflation is low or practically nonexistent, the farmer is quite willing to receive 3 or 4 percent interest on this money and the person borrowing the money is quite content to pay 6 to 7 percent for its use. But when inflation rises, as it has during the past twenty years, interest rates also rise. The farmer who has deposited his $1,000, seeing that inflation now runs 8 percent a year, knows that just keeping his money even in purchasing power will require an 8 percent interest rate. To actually make money, he will need 10 to 11 percent. Since the bank has to make a profit too, it will now charge a borrower 13 to 14 percent. The cost of capital has become high.

But there is another way capital can become expensive, and this is through inflation itself. If interest rates are high, capital is expensive to borrow, and money not earning those high rates loses value when compared with money that is. Inflation also reflects the cost of capital because as prices rise, the value of money declines, so that to hold money during inflation is to see its value decrease. Its "expense" was the cost of seeing it go down in value, from $1,000, let us say, to only $900 in one year. This is why people are apt to spend their money during inflation on property or goods, to see its value stay even or even get ahead of the inflation rate. As shown in Table 3, both inflation and interest rates have increased dramatically during the past two decades. The question is: Why?

Neither high interest rates nor high inflation is desirable, but both have occurred despite efforts to the contrary. Anyone who has read about the economy during the past decade has read dozens of articles and explanations: inflation is caused by OPEC, indexing, labor demands, falling productivity, overexpansion of the money supply under Presidents Carter and Ford, and too much consumption linked with too little savings; high interest rates have been blamed on the government's tax policies, the "inflation premium" demanded by lenders afraid of future inflation, Paul Volcker and the Federal Reserve Board, falling productivity, OPEC oil price shocks rippling through the system, budget deficits, and the supply-side economic policies of the Reagan administration.

These explanations are only partly true because they miss the central cause. The high cost of capital is caused by the decline of the mass economy. Inflation and high interest rates, alternating from one decade to the next, are both the symptoms and the causes of the decline. What we have done during the past decade is increase our debt instead of our capital. To ease the consequences of the lack of real economic growth in the mass economy, we have borrowed instead of invested. Individuals, corporations, and governments have all increased their debt to staggering amounts. While some of this debt has gone into new capital investments, most has gone into the consumption of goods. Over 97 percent of our GNP during the 1970s was consumed—only 2¼ percent was reinvested. While increased spending has covered up, for the short run, the contraction of the mass economy, it has weakened the economy further because much of it has been financed through increased debt. Unless there is an economic collapse, the cost of capital will remain high as we make the transition from the mass economy to the informative economy. Increased debt will continue to divert a substantial portion of our national income to debt service, paying the interest and principal on our debt, rather than to capital investment.

The mass economy cannot grow because of the

Table 3*

Time Period	Inflation Rate	Interest Rate on Moody's AAA Bonds
1925	0.2%	5.0%
1930	−2.5	4.5
1935	2.5	3.6
1940	1.0	2.8
1945	2.3	2.6
1950	1.0	2.6
1955	−0.4	3.1
1960	1.6	4.4
1965	1.7	4.5
1970	5.9	8.0
1975	9.1	8.8
1976	5.8	8.4
1977	6.5	8.0
1978	7.6	8.7
1979	11.3	9.6
1980	13.5	11.9
1981	10.4	14.2
1982	3.9	12.0

* Rates compiled from information in Value Line.

changing ratio of values among labor, capital, and energy. The basic historical trend, going back to the late nineteenth century, had labor go up in value, resources become cheaper, and capital become increasingly available. Labor became more expensive as a growing, more complex mass economy demanded an increasing variety of skills while it lowered the real cost of goods through increased productivity. Because of energy's relative abundance and the enormously increased ease with which it was extracted and distributed, its cost went down as demand for it rose. The growth of capital during the expansion of the mass economy was a direct result of the prosperity that our economic system gained through the injection of energy. Primarily in the form of oil, this energy increased our ability to produce goods, lowered their real costs, created wealth and growth, and thus provided us with new capital and a high standard of living.

As the cost of energy climbed sharply after OPEC's actions in 1973, economic expansion reversed. Energy, the primary mechanism for increasing productivity, became more expensive than the productivity gains it made possible. Using more energy didn't save money or help produce less expensive goods; rather, the increased use of energy cost more money and made goods more expensive.

As the new cost of energy made itself felt throughout the economy, profits declined, the growth of wages slowed, and consumers cut back on buying. Although the economy recovered from the 1973 oil shock and grew moderately between 1976 and 1978, the second oil shock, brought about by the revolution in Iran in 1979, launched a second economic dislocation. Without growth, the amount of new capital available for investment declined.

As I noted earlier, capital, because it represents real wealth, can be invested in an economic system to create new productive capacity and jobs. Although capital can take the form of money, the mere issuance of money does not mean it is capital. This fact, well known to economists, was contradicted by Keynesian economic theory. Beginning with Franklin Roosevelt's administration and until the election of Ronald Reagan, the dominant theory guiding the U.S. economy came from the work of the British economist John Maynard Keynes (1883–1946). Keynes stated in his book *The General Theory of Employment, Interest and Money* that government could effectively manage the economy by either stimulating or restricting the demand for goods through fiscal or budgetary means—hence the term *demand-side economics*. He thought that if under certain circumstances an otherwise healthy economy could not generate enough demand to maintain high production and employment, it would become the government's duty to increase demand artificially by cutting taxes without cutting government spending or by raising government spending without raising taxes. In other words, the government would raise demand by going into debt. If the economy became too heated and inflation began, the government could reverse the process by reducing spending, raising taxes, or both. While attempts to raise industrial production and employment before World War II by following Keynesian principles did not seem to produce the results predicted, they worked extremely well during the long period of growth after World War II. By the 1960s Keynesian policies had reached their finest hour, and businessmen and economists talked of a new era of steady growth and management of the economy through the "fine-tuning" made possible by Keynesian theory.

Since 1974, however, Keynesian theory has not predicted or eased the turn of economic events. Demand-side manipulation was a system imposed on society by the government, but the economy resisted the theory because it knows what Keynesian theory does not: economic growth cannot be fueled by debt and, further, the underlying principles of economic growth have changed. The economy since World War II has been driven by cheap energy. Although the markets have adjusted to the rising cost of energy, Keynesian theories, formulated during a period of falling energy prices, have not.

When President Ford took office in 1974, the country was trying to recover from the political shock of Nixon's resignation and the worst recession since the Depression. In keeping with Keynesian policy, President Ford's first budget increased the operating deficit of the government from $11 billion in 1974 to $75 billion in 1975. This policy of fiscal stimulation was continued the next year and thereafter by President Carter during his four years in office. Although both presidents would have preferred balanced budgets, they were more concerned about stimulating the economy and reducing unemployment. The purpose of these deficits was to shore up the mass economy, reduce the cost of energy by encouraging new development and exploration, strengthen the support for those on the bottom rungs of the economy, compensate the unemployed until they could get back to work, and generally restimulate a pattern of growth that would increase government revenues and lower deficits. It didn't work out that way.

In order to grasp the enormity of this six-year plunge into deficits, it is useful to compare the twenty-six-year period between the election of Harry Truman and the resignation of President Nixon with the succeeding six-year period during the Ford and Carter administrations. Between 1948 and 1974 national debt increased from $214 billion to $351 billion, an increase of $137 billion or 64 percent. In the next six years, debt increased by $386 billion—110 percent—to $737 billion. Another way to look at this difference is to compare the net borrowing of the federal government during a six-year period in two consecutive decades, as shown in Table 4.

Table 4

Year	Net Borrowing	Year	Net Borrowing
1965	$ 4.06 billion	1975	$ 85.49 billion
1966	3.08	1976	69.03
1967	2.84	1977	56.81
1968	5.42	1978	53.69
1969	−2.55	1979	37.37
1970	11.86	1980	79.20
	$ 25.81		$381.59

According to Keynesian theory, the level of debt is supposed to go up or down in relation to the rise or fall of economic activity. As a business cycle heats up and economic expansion accelerates, debt usually increases faster than the rate of economic growth, as consumers borrow to make purchases and businesses borrow to increase manufacturing capacity. When the economy slows down and growth declines, debt is reduced at a faster rate than the rate at which the economy is contracting, as consumers and businesses stop spending and try to lower expenses. Like the pumping of water into the locks of a canal, debt lifts us into new levels of economic activity and then declines to an acceptable level. But this clearly has not happened. Throughout the seventies and into the eighties, debt of all kinds has continued to grow at a rapid rate.

There is no intention here to undercut Keynesian economic theories or to push other theories that supposedly would have worked better. The fact is that virtually every industrialized economy showed tremendous growth and prosperity between the end of World War II and 1973, regardless of what economic theory dominated the thinking of individual governments. The economy succeeded for other reasons, ones very different from theory, and it has failed not because of theory but because its structural foundations have been shaken by the shift in the relationships among labor, capital, and energy.

When the government increases its national debt, it is borrowing money and promising to pay it back later. Who lends money to the government? Just about everyone: commercial banks, foreigners, small savers, and the government itself through the Federal Reserve Bank. When the government borrows money from the private sector and spends it on government purchases, this is money that is not otherwise available for lending to businesses. In other words, capital is withdrawn from productive investments and placed in the hands of government, where it is used almost exclusively for consumption: Social Security, welfare, missiles, Medicare, and so on. In order to accommodate the needs of the government during the 1970s, the Federal Reserve Bank increased the money supply in the hope that the United States could have both fiscal stimulation through government deficits and increased capital investment for future economic growth.

But because money and capital are not synonymous, increasing the supply of money does not increase the supply of capital. To understand this, it is necessary to know how money is created. While the Congress and the Treasury can create debt, the Federal Reserve Bank can create money. Technically, money is created by the nation's banks, but their ability to do this is regulated by the Federal Reserve Bank. Money is created by the constant relending of bank deposits. For example, suppose our farmer borrows $50,000 to buy a tractor. He goes to the bank, borrows the money, and pays the dealer, who promptly puts the money back in the bank—for the sake of this example, the same bank. The bank can now reloan the money—the new $50,000 deposit—to another farmer who wants to buy a tractor. The second farmer borrows the money, pays the dealer, and the dealer promptly deposits the money into the bank again. The money supply has doubled. To control this growth, the Federal Reserve Bank sets requirements for the percentage of deposits a bank must hold in reserve. A second way the Federal Reserve can increase the supply of money is to purchase Treasury bills from member banks or from the Treasury itself. When the Treasury wants to borrow money, the Fed can write the Treasury a check. The Treasury deposits this check in a bank, and the bank presents the check back to the Federal Reserve Bank. The Fed credits the bank with new reserves that it can use as a basis for making new loans. A third way the supply of money can be increased or decreased is through the discount rate, the interest rate at which member banks of the Federal Reserve can borrow money from the Fed. This rate can be lowered to stimulate borrowing or raised to discourage it.

Between 1933 and 1967, the annual growth of the money supply in the United States averaged 4 percent. The growth of money then climbed to between 7 and 8 percent per year during the Carter administration. Economists say that inflation results when the annual growth of the money supply consistently exceeds the rate of growth in gross national product, the nation's total output of goods and services. For example, during the past fifty years our gross national product has increased six times. During that period, our supply of money has increased twenty-five times. This means there is four times as much money chasing our goods as there was fifty years ago, and, not surprisingly, the price of goods during the past fifty years has risen nearly five times.

The combination of large fiscal deficits and an expanding monetary supply during the 1970s created an inflationary environment that crested at 18 percent during the first quarter of 1980. This stimulated increased borrowing and widespread speculation that made inflation worse and decreased real capital investment. When inflation is rising and currency is falling in value, the sensible thing to do is get out of currency and buy something that will rise with the tide of inflation. Furthermore, when money is declining in value it seems to make more sense to borrow money, because repayment will be in cheaper, discounted dollars.

If the only increase in debt was the federal debt, we would have no problem servicing it. Unfortunately, other areas of the economy have increased debt at an even faster rate than the federal government. Between 1950 and 1980 federal debt rose by approximately 300 percent, while consumer debt rose 1,300 percent, mortgages 1,500 percent, corporate debt 1,200 percent, and state and local government 1,300 percent. When the economy was growing consistently, we worried about the ability of the nation to service its debt, whether consumer, corporate, or government. But debt has been increasing and continues to grow faster than the nominal rate of economic growth. In 1951 the amount of debt for every $1 of gross national product was $1.31. By 1978 it had climbed to $1.58 and in 1982 was climbing still. (See Table 5.)

Table 5

TOTAL DEBT OWED BY NONFINANCIAL SECTORS*

Year	GNP	Debt	Percent
1951	330.2	432.9	131
1955	399.3	556.2	139
1960	506.0	737.6	146
1965	688.1	1025.8	149
1970	982.4	1453.7	148
1975	1528.8	2351.7	154
1978	2127.6	3351.4	158

* These figures exclude banks, insurance, etc., and are calculated in billions of dollars and as percentage of GNP.

While this increase of 27 percent in the ratio of debt to production may seem small, it has a much larger impact when specific aspects of the economy are examined. As the amount of money required to service debt increases, less money is available for investment and, as growth slows, the more difficult it becomes for the economy to meet all of its debts. As greater demands are placed on existing capital to pay debt, interest rates go up, making the expense of carrying debt even more punitive to everyone. For example, consumer debt service—the total payments made on mortgages and installment loans—was less than 5 percent of disposable income in 1945, and the average interest rate paid was 6 percent. By 1965 the average rate of interest was 10 percent and debt service was using up 22 percent of disposable income. By 1979 interest rates had climbed to 16 percent and consumer debt service required 29 percent of disposable income.

The story is similar in the corporate world. There, the ratio of interest payments to after-tax profits reveals that more of what corporations earn must be used to repay debt instead of being available for reinvestment or distribution to shareholders. Corporations are "purchasing" growth and earnings by going more deeply into debt. As shown in Table 6, the ratio of interest to profits has climbed from a low of 9.3 percent in 1950 to 163.4 percent in 1981.

This rise in debt will be made worse by the Reagan administration budgets, which increase expenditures from $742 billion in fiscal year 1982 to $1.01 trillion in 1985. More than $750 billion of new deficits will be incurred during this period, bringing the total federal deficit to $1.75 trillion. Interest payments on the national debt already total more than $100 billion a year and are the third greatest budget expense after Social Security and the military. If deficits grow as projected, the government, starting in 1983, will require more than 100 percent of all new savings to finance its net bor-

Table 6

Year	Net Interest*	After-tax Profits	Percent
1950	2.3 billion	24.7 billion	9.3
1955	4.8	26.4	18.2
1960	9.8	25.8	38.0
1965	18.5	44.3	41.8
1970	37.5	37.0	101.3
1975	79.1	73.4	107.7
1979	141.8	130.5	108.7
1980	170.9	127.5	134.0
1981	209.3	128.1	163.4

* Net interest equals interest paid minus interest received.

rowings. Meanwhile, it has accumulated liabilities not reflected in the budget deficits that total $5 trillion, consisting of loan guarantees, pension commitments, insurance liabilities, and unfunded Social Security liabilities. These off-budget liabilities, when combined with the present total national debt of approximately $5 trillion, mean that we owe ourselves $10 trillion. We simply don't have the money and won't be able to pay it.

When President Reagan was elected, the number-one problem in the economy was inflation; unemployment was second. Before Reagan's election, President Carter appointed Paul Volcker chairman of the Federal Reserve Board in order to quell criticism that his administration was too liberal in its monetary policies and to restore confidence in the financial markets, which were near panic in 1979. Volcker abruptly changed the long-standing policy of the Federal Reserve of monetizing substantial portions of the national debt by having the Federal Reserve "buy" portions of the debt from the Treasury Department. These purchases, while reducing the amount of total debt needed to be financed by the private sector, also had the effect of expanding the supply of money in the banking system.

Volcker began a policy of restricting the growth of the money supply while allowing interest rates to find their own market level. Before this, the Fed, through its discount rate, supplied funds to banks at rates of interest that varied with its monetary policy. In this way, the Fed kept a lid on interest rates while the monetization of debt, prior to Volcker's tenure, also prevented these rates from rising much higher than the rate of inflation itself.

Volcker's intention was to bring inflation under control, and by 1982 it had been cut by more than two-thirds, to 3.9 percent, from its 1980 rate of 13.5 percent. But as inflation dropped, unemployment rose to over 10 percent, the highest rate since the Depression. High interest rates had reduced consumer spending and sent scores of businesses into bankruptcy and caused hundreds of thousands of workers to be laid off.

As the economy continued to weaken through late 1982, interest rates began to subside somewhat, but "real" interest rates—the difference between the rate of inflation and the rate of interest paid on high-quality, long-term bonds—remained the highest in over fifty years, at 7 to 8 percent instead of the normal 2 to 3 percent. The reason interest rates began to subside was simple: in August 1982, the Federal Reserve began monetizing debt again by placing reserves in the economy. Once again it began to purchase Treasury debt as well as lower the discount rate on funds lent to member banks. The economy was weaker than had been thought, and the government was fearful of economic collapse.

We are confronted, then, with a series of unpleasant choices. As debt has increased over the past decades faster than the rate of economic growth, it has increased the demand for cash and raised interest rates to historic highs. If the government meets the demand

The Next Economy

for money by rapidly increasing the money supply, it creates inflation and a new upward spiraling of debt as individuals and businesses try to borrow. If, instead, the government clamps down on the money supply, the economy is weakened and its ability to repay debt diminishes. At the same time, the nation's need for new debt increases in order to keep afloat during economic contraction. In the words of a pessimistic governor of the Federal Reserve Board, we are "between Scylla and Charybdis.... You can push the economy so hard to kill inflation that you discourage business and there is no investment.... You get the anti-inflationary effects but not any expansionary effects and if you ease you get...inflation again.... No one is a winner." So no matter what policy the Fed pursues, the cost of capital will remain high.

We are in an economy that requires more debt to survive but whose ability to sustain that debt is declining. The last time the United States had high consumer, mortgage, agricultural, and corporate debts as well as cash-poor countries owing large amounts to U.S. banks was in 1929. What happened then was a classic credit collapse. The structure of debt that had been built up could no longer be sustained by the economy, and a long painful period of deflation and liquidation took place that devastated the country for a decade: one-fourth of all jobs were lost, ten thousand banks failed, the gross national product dropped by 50 percent, and wages dropped by a third. If these parallels are not a sufficient reminder, there was an eerie one in a September 1982 *Wall Street Journal* column entitled "Business Bulletin."

Wall Street's next message for customers: Go into Hock.

Several big brokerage firms will soon mount campaigns to increase customer borrowing. Col-

lecting interest can be a better source of profit
than commissions, the firms have long since
learned. And the Securities and Exchange Commission recently halved—to 2 percent—the portion of customer debt that a firm must match with
reserve capital; the firms thus could do twice as
much lending without tying up more funds. Currently, Wall Street customers owe about $14 bil-
lion in margin debt; that figure could triple in a
year or so if the stock market is strong, says
Sanford I. Weill, chairman of Shearson/American
Express.

E. F. Hutton coaches brokers in the fine art
of coaxing customers to borrow; both Shearson
and Merrill Lynch consider a propaganda blitz of
mailings. Wall Street marketers worry, though,
that the term "margin" evokes images of risk,
bursting bubbles and the like; a salable euphe-
mism is sought.

"We're studying all sorts of lily-flower
phrases," says George Ball, Hutton's President.

Merrill Lynch has an even better idea. It is creating
an Equity Access account where individuals can dip
in and out of their home equity as easily as picking up
the phone. Like other brokerage houses, it has tried
to come up with a way to take the stigma out of debt—
in this case, the second mortgage. Customers with an
Equity Access account can charge expenses to their
house with their Visa card. And what will people do
with the money? That's a touchy subject because, technically, a securities broker cannot offer a loan to persons to buy stocks or bonds. But this is a law that is
not enforceable. Once the money is received, how can
it be distinguished from other funds? What Merrill
Lynch, E. F. Hutton, and other brokers fail to mention
is how this expansion of consumer credit is going to

help either the economy or the consumer. The newspapers are full of stories of corporations, even nations, that have badly overextended themselves using easy credit access. Are we to become a nation of "savvy" individuals all following the conventional wisdom of becoming "leveraged" when all around us is the evidence of such folly—deflation, contraction, and illiquidity?

A similar effort by lenders fed the speculative binge in stockmarket trading that led to the collapse on Black Tuesday in 1929. This "call money" was available from numerous sources besides brokers at rates from 10 to 20 percent. So lucrative was the loaning of call money that funds from all over the world poured into New York to be loaned to speculators, fueling the stockmarket rally and making its eventual collapse worse than it might otherwise have been.

I do not think we will see a repetition of Black Tuesday or of 1929. Yet few adults alive today have a working memory of the events that led up to the credit collapse and the Depression, so it is useful to remind ourselves that spiraling debt and ignorance of its consequences have always precipitated financial panics, collapses, and depressions throughout the world. I have faith that we can extricate ourselves from the dilemma of soaring debt and expensive capital costs. But it won't be done by inventing "lily-flower phrases" that inspire deeper indebtedness. It will be done slowly and carefully by realizing that much of our supposed wealth does not exist, that the United States will require a long period of restrained consumption, increased production, and self-reliance in order to reduce debt to manageable levels. There is no way to predict whether the future will bring disinflation (the downward movement of inflation rates) and high interest rates, renewed inflation, or both, because such developments are rooted in political decisions. We may well alternate in whipsaw fashion from one to the other or suffer a decade of grinding liquidation of our debt, which would mean severe economic dislocation, insolvency, and economic restructuring. Either way, the greatest flexibility is gained by not being in debt.

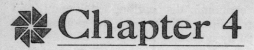

Chapter 4

The Long
Contraction

According to the government, the U.S. gross national product, when adjusted for inflation, increased 19 percent between 1973 and 1981, an annual increase of just over 2 percent. Because of this statistic we assume we live in a growing economy.

The gross national product is the total production of goods and services measured by either purchases or sales. In compiling the index only final purchases of sales are counted, not the intermediate steps or exchanges. These final transactions consist of four components: consumer purchases, including house payments and improvements; investments by business; government expenditures; and the difference between exports and imports. The total of these four is adjusted for inflation during the year, and the "real" economic growth is computed. But we are not growing—we are contracting. Our reliance on statistics is blinding us to what is happening.

To say that the GNP has gone up 2 percent in one year is like the weatherman saying that the mean U.S. temperature rose .0035 degrees centigrade yesterday. It may be true, but it doesn't tell you whether you should have a picnic or wear a raincoat. Similarly, because the GNP is a "gross" figure it measures *everything* purchased and makes no distinction between a car, a Coke, and a creation. It is a measure of our transactions (at least the reported ones), but it is not necessarily a measure of growth. In order for an economy to grow, its capacity to produce wealth must grow. This requires saving income by delaying consumption and then investing these savings in making our human and physical resources productive. Because the mass economy is an extractive economy, the bulk of the GNP measures what we extract—trees cut, iron melted, hamburgers eaten. This is fine as far as it goes—economic activity is intimately involved with using up resources—but it does not reveal whether we are living off principal or interest. Principal is our capital and natural resources: factories, farms, forests, waterways, and so on. Interest is what we are taking from these resources—steel, corn, lumber, and water. Equally important is *monetary* principal and interest. If we are merely creating more money through debt, we are not growing but instead are setting up a long and painful process of liquidation that does not reveal itself while debt expands. An economy that expands its debt faster than it increases output grows only as long as society is willing and able to create and service new debt. If either the willingness or ability should falter, even momentarily, an economy can collapse.

If we are living off principal, we are contracting. I have known heirs who lived off their inheritances for many years. Their lives remained unchanged right up until bankruptcy. Though that may be a crude analogy for the complexity of our economy, it points to the central problem of using the GNP as a measure of economic growth. The GNP measures primarily what we spend. If we spend more by borrowing more, we are gaining a short-term sense of growth in exchange for a long-term postponement of reconciling our debts with our assets. The total wealth of the United States, from real estate to stocks, from gold fillings to the last piece of silverware, amounts to $7 to $8 trillion. It is also estimated that we now owe $5.2 trillion against that. If the United States was a business, it would have difficulty getting a loan.

Because the GNP does not distinguish between expenditures, it includes those that are a direct result of economic contraction. When International Harvester lays off 5,000 workers, they collect company, union, and government benefits, the spending of which registers as economic activity. Crime rises during periods of unemployment, as do alcoholism, child abuse, and mental disorder. The increased purchases of liquor, stepped-up police activity, and psychiatric treatment are shown as economic growth. So is the handgun bought by the fearful person.

The case of the Manville Corporation is another example of how conventional government accounting ignores real economic contraction. When it filed in the fall of 1982 for reorganization under Chapter 11 of the Federal Bankruptcy Code, Manville's chief executive officer, John McKinney, said, "Nothing is wrong with our business." While literally whistling past the graveyard, the Manville Corporation, for forty years the leading manufacturer of products containing asbestos, has been sued by 16,500 plaintiffs for damages resulting from deaths and injuries, primarily lung cancer, that allegedly occurred as employees of the firm or workers in other industries such as shipbuilding were exposed to asbestos. There is something wrong with Manville's business, something that a Manville-commissioned study estimates to have affected at least 52,000 people in a crippling manner. In an interview put out by Manville's corporate relations department, McKinney said he felt "awful" because "loyal suppliers" and shareholders may "suffer losses."

Manville's actions reflect the limitations of the mass economy and illustrate a form of economic contraction. An economic philosophy that stresses physical growth (mass) at the potential expense of learning (information) is now being challenged by the many people and their relatives who have suffered. Although Manville and the various litigants heatedly dispute the point at which Manville became aware of the dangers of asbestos, at some time some doubt of its safety to humans must have occurred to officers of the corporation. Did they cease asbestos-related activities at that point? Claims amounting to over $2 billion now lie at Manville's door, but instead of trying to deal with them, Manville has turned the matter over to the courts, letting suppliers, creditors, and taxpayers figure out who is going to pay for the damages. This illustrates how much of past growth has yet to be paid for. Whatever happens, the medical and legal expenses relating to asbestos exposure will increase the gross national product—hardly a measure of real growth.

Asbestos products were cheap on the one hand and very expensive on the other. By being cheaply made they exposed workers and others to asbestos fibers for decades. Because of initial cheapness, they will cost a fortune later. One of the paradoxes of the mass economy is that by producing so much so inexpensively, it brought on its own demise. Because the ratio of mass to information was so much in favor of mass consumption, cars tended to guzzle gas, houses were overheated, and many goods quickly wore out.

Essentially the mass economy made less with more, and those industries now contracting the most are the ones that were the most wasteful in the past.

In the mass economy after World War II, automobiles were made not to be economical but to satisfy needs other than transportation. Cars were overbuilt, overpowered, and expensive to run, and their safety was underengineered. As high energy costs have permeated the U.S. economy, people have bought more cars manufactured in Europe and Japan, where energy has been expensive and valued for a long time. For the domestic auto industry, the 1982 sales year was the worst in twenty-four years. But U.S. sales were at a record high for imported cars—28 percent of sales. In the bellwether state of California, imports now account for nearly 50 percent of new car sales.

The U.S. housing industry, at its lowest level since World War II, is in no better shape. Sixty percent of all builders have gone out of business, and housing-related jobs have shrunk by 2 million. After World War II, housing became airier, larger, more luxurious. The average size of a new house went from 1,100 square feet in 1950 to 2,100 square feet in 1980. Our housing stock was inexpensive to build, given our abundant resources of wood, land, and capital. During the three decades following the war, new housing construction expanded. But as energy, building materials, and capital have become expensive, so have houses. We may want big houses but we can no longer afford them— used or new. "It is the same phenomenon that we are seeing in autos," says economist Robert Sinche. "People are maintaining their homes longer and maintaining them better." In the meantime, many who did buy houses during the past few years are having difficulty keeping them. It is estimated that the Bank of America now has 20,000 houses that can be foreclosed upon but doesn't know what it would do with them. Nationwide, 140,000 homes were in foreclosure as of June 1982, the highest number of defaulted loans since records began to be kept thirty years ago.

The American steel industry was running at less than 40 percent capacity in the third quarter of 1982, its lowest figure since 1938, and steel mills laid off 130,000 workers during the past three years. Because of the availability of cheap energy, the U.S. steel industry retained the older, less-efficient electric hearth mills instead of investing in continuous casting methods that would have made plants more energy- and labor-efficient. Steel producers throughout the world have been affected by reduced demand, but the United States, with its high energy and labor costs, has been hurt the most. With labor costs 50 percent higher than in Japan and imports reaching 24 percent of the U.S. market, something must give. Since energy costs are fixed, it will have to be labor. If labor won't give, the industry will contract further.

In all three industries the extravagant use of energy and materials before 1973 allowed greater consumption and produced greater demand than if energy and resources had been expensive. Now that energy is expensive, extravagance changes to frugality, and few like it. As costs go up, consumption and profits go down. As profits fall, investment falls. As investment falls, debt rises. As debt rises, costs go up and consumer purchases fall further. This spiraling down of the mass economy unfolds into economic contraction.

Here are other examples of contraction:

Unemployment: The 11 million Americans who are unemployed must wonder how it is that the GNP has grown while their numbers have risen. Many are in the process of liquidating their assets in order to live, and yet their drop in net worth does not show as a loss. As they go into debt, spend their savings on food, and in some cases spend the proceeds from the sale of their houses, their activity is recorded as part of the GNP. More ominous for long-term economic health is that unemployment levels do not fall back to their pre-recession levels after every "recovery." During the Vietnam War, unemployment was below 4 percent; during the 1971–73 recovery, unemployment fell to below 5 percent. During the 1976–79 recovery, unemployment briefly fell under 6 percent; after the 1980 recession, it never went lower than 7.2 percent. By the end of 1982, unemployment stood at 10.8 percent, and it was still rising. The 11 million people who are not working are joined by 5.5 million people who would like to work full-time but can get only part-time work and by another 1.7 million people who have stopped looking for work—so-called discouraged workers. Although much media attention is devoted to the unemployment rate among teen-agers—24 percent for whites, 49 percent for blacks—an even grimmer statistic was reported in September 1982 by Congressman Claude Pepper, chairman of the House Select Committee on Aging: nearly one-fourth of all people over fifty-five who want to work are unemployed. These are people who have worked for years in such male-dominated industries as consumer durables and steel, rubber, and automobile manufacture. Their job prospects are far worse than a teen-ager's because these industries are shrinking. Unemployment comes to them when they most need income for retirement and savings.

Infrastructure: The GNP records the making of a bridge and the paving of a road, but it does not register the bridge's decay. The mass economy created an immense system of roads, interstate highways, aqueducts, and bridges. During the expansionary phase of the mass economy this buildup of public works added greatly to employment and prosperity. Now these works are wearing out, and we may not have the money to maintain them:

> The Transportation Department has estimated that it will require $47 billion to repair or replace the more than 250,000 obsolete or decaying bridges in the nation.
> It will require $700 billion to maintain the secondary roads in the next ten years.
> Although the 42,000-mile interstate highway system is not yet completed, it needs to be rebuilt at the rate of 2,000 miles per year, and there is already an 8,000-mile backlog.
> New York State estimates its requirements for public works maintenance at $8 billion to $10 billion per year.
> According to *The New York Times*, "New York City alone over the next few years would have to service, repair or replace 1,000 bridges, two aqueducts, one large water tunnel, several reservoirs, 6,200 miles of streets, 6,000 miles of sewers, 6,000 miles of water lines, 6,700 subway cars, 4,500 buses, 25,000 acres of parks, 17 hospitals, 19 city university campuses, 950 schools, 200 libraries and several hundred fire houses and police stations."

The total bill over the next decade is put at $3 trillion, or just under 10 percent of the gross national product. We are now spending less than 2 percent of GNP on public works, which itself reflects a 60 percent drop since 1965.

Paper Losses: In constant 1975 dollars, the gross national product grew from $1.80 trillion in 1978 to $1.86

trillion in 1979, a 3 percent rise. In contrast, if the assets
represented by all of the mortgages and bonds held by
institutions and individuals had been reported at their
market value at the end of 1979, there would have been
$700 billion in paper losses, caused by rising interest
rates—the greatest financial crash in history. The bulk
of these paper losses was incurred by pension funds
and life-insurance companies.

Losses have also been incurred by thrift institutions, which in 1981 held about $800 billion worth of
mortgages. Unlike you and me, they report the value
of these holdings at the price they paid for them. If
your shares of General Motors stock goes down, you
show that on a statement of net worth. In the case of
thrift institutions, the value of their mortgages has declined sharply, yet they are not required to report this
change in the underlying value of their assets. If the
savings and loan industries reported the actual value
of their mortgages, they would be closer to $550 billion.
This means that every dollar deposited in a savings
and loan in 1981 was backed by about 70 cents in
assets. Against potential depositor losses, the Federal
Savings & Loan Insurance Corporation (FSLIC) has
reserves of $6.3 billion, down from $34 billion in 1981.
At present the FSLIC is merging insolvent savings and
loans with solvent ones, hoping to forestall payments
to depositors. Why would a solvent savings and loan
want to merge with one that is virtually bankrupt? The
FSLIC allows the solvent partner in the merger to write
off his losses over thirty years while reporting the gain
in assets immediately. This type of creative accounting, which would be called fraudulent if a business did
it, is justified by the FSLIC because more conservative
accounting would cripple the industry.

Utilities: Many utilities are able to continue paying stock
dividends only by borrowing the money for them from

their banks and customers. In the past ten years utilities have increased their debt by tens of billions of dollars primarily in order to build nuclear power plants. Now the utilities are having trouble meeting their debts. During the fifties and sixties, declining fuel prices together with increasingly efficient technology enabled utilities to produce electric power more cheaply even as demand rose rapidly—the "golden years," according to W. C. Tallman, chairman of the Public Service Company of New Hampshire. In 1974, the higher oil prices set by OPEC began to take hold and utilities found themselves with declining cash even after large rate hikes. To accommodate the new era of rising energy costs, the utilities began construction on larger power plants, most of which were nuclear. But two things happened. As electricity rates soared, customers cut back, particularly after the 1979 oil price hike. At the same time, both the cost of capital and the cost for new construction rose dramatically. The utilities now find themselves with expensive, half-finished power plants financed by large, high-interest bonds but without sufficient demand to justify completing the plants.

The utilities are caught between realizing they have made large financial mistakes and pretending their customers need electricity they don't want. To meet their new debt, utilities have had to borrow more and seek additional rate increases. This, in turn, has inspired customers to even more vigorous cutting back on energy use through weather-stripping, conservation, and household insulation.

In order to maintain earnings growth even as cash flow and earnings fall, utilities have had to adopt peculiar accounting methods. They can now receive credits for still incomplete power plants and add them to their profits. These credits, known as the "allowance for funds used during construction," accounted for 14 percent of utilities' earnings in 1979 and for nearly 50 percent in 1980.

There is no business that better typifies the peaking of the mass economy than utilities. As they grow, they contract. The contraction is papered over by creative accounting and massive borrowing. For many, future salvation is attainable only if the use of electrical energy rapidly grows. Because many of the power plants stalled by financing problems are nuclear plants, Charles Dean, chairman of the Tennessee Valley Authority (TVA), has called for a $50 billion bailout of the nuclear power industry. This would create a national nuclear energy pool that would purchase the uncompleted nuclear reactors from the utilities and finish them. But that is not growth. And that's the problem with the mass economy. Chairman Dean of the TVA is not talking about real economic growth; he is talking about saving face, about subsidizing an economic system that even by its own admission does not translate into real profits. The federal government has already subsidized the nuclear energy industry with $35 billion of taxpayers' funds over the past thirty years.

During the same decade that nuclear fuel was foundering, wood fuel surpassed nuclear reactors as a source of energy, and it didn't require a cent of taxpayers' money. Wood stoves are more economical than nuclear power plants, and individuals have been more than willing to make that kind of investment. Utilities have unwillingly learned how to create more power—raise the prices. Every time they do, we use less electricity, making available new power.

A unique and fascinating way to look at overall contraction is through what financial columnist Scott Burns calls the "Barrel Standard." Instead of using dollars, Burns measures the value of companies on the New York Stock Exchange in barrels of oil. The process gives a startling view of values and reinforces the notion that we are seeing a dramatic shift in the relationships among energy, capital, and labor.

For example, buying one share each of all the Dow Jones thirty industrial stocks would have cost 556 barrels in 1970. In late 1982, with the Dow Jones still around 1,000, as it was in the early 1970s, it would have cost 30 barrels—a drop of 95 percent. Individual stocks, including AT&T, IBM, and Coca-Cola, showed similar 95 percent drops in value over the decade when measured against the price of oil. Since we don't buy goods with oil but with money, what does this mean? It signifies deflation. While during the seventies the world economy experienced a monetary inflation powered by the oil price rises, the underlying value of capital assets was dropping sharply downward.

Is it fair to measure value in oil? Absolutely, because it is oil and similar energy equivalents that supply us with the work that makes modern life possible. When such an enormous shift occurs in the relationship between oil and what it fuels—business and industry—there is also a fundamental revaluation of labor and capital. We have tried to cover this change in value with more money, causing inflation and/or high interest rates. Neither will maintain the standard of living achieved by industrial society, and in the meantime the economy declines and contracts.

What has kept the American economy alive in the years following 1973 is spending, not investments. Most of the spending was done by consumers and reflects their response to inflation—to buy something of enduring value with their weakening dollar. Because the government's policy during the 1970s was to inject reserves into the monetary system, consumers responded by buying houses, cars, and other durable goods. However, this spending reduced the amount of savings available for capital investment. If there is a credit collapse or a sudden major default of debt by a sovereign nation, the economy may be too weak to recover, revealing in the process that its underlying strength has been eroding for nearly a decade.

Economic contraction occurs when levels of production and consumption cannot be sustained. Economic collapse occurs when economic contraction coincides with a period of excessive buildup of debt. It is preceded by a period in which debt climbs quickly in the hope that each new level of indebtedness will finally see the economy "turn around" and service the debt. The collapse is the realization that it won't work. There is a crisis of confidence. People panic, sell stocks, call notes, liquidate holdings, and rush to currency or instruments that have value.

The world has experienced three severe economic collapses since the beginning of the nineteenth century. The last was in 1929 and had been predicted by a Marxist economist, Nikolai Kondratieff, in a book published in 1926 entitled *The Long Waves in Economic Life*.

Kondratieff's theories evolved from his study of commodity prices. As he tracked prices in France, the United States, and Britain, he noticed that they rose and fell with long, sweeping regularity and that the periods from peak to peak were strikingly regular— from fifty to sixty years. The peaks and troughs of the long waves are shown in Table 7.

Economists are divided on the validity of the long-wave theory. Some ascribe no more credibility to Kondratieff than they would to mysticism or astrology, because it doesn't fit into any disciplined or empirical framework. Others, including the prominent economists Jay Forrester of MIT and the late Austrian-American Joseph Schumpeter, are not so sure. Schumpeter believed that long cycles of prosperity and depression were caused by new technologies and products that set off a wave of investment and growth that would peak when the change effected by the new technology was complete. Under this interpretation, the last wave, starting after World War II, is ascribed to the automobile, and this cycle is said to have reached its peak with the rise of oil prices in 1973.

Table 7

Trough	Peak	Length (peak to peak)
1789	1814	
1849	1864	50 years
1896	1920	56 years
1946	1973	53 years

Jay Forrester independently confirmed a long wave when he established a computerized model of the economy based on the production and consumption of capital goods. Forrester says that our present economy closely resembles conditions found at the peak of a long wave. He writes, "At such a peak one should expect a decline in new capital investment, rising unemployment, a leveling out in labor productivity, high interest rates, rising prices, falling return on investment, increasing amplitude of business cycles and reduced innovation from maturing of the current wave of technological advance. Such conditions fit today's situation. Similar conditions last occurred in the 1920s at the previous long-wave peak."

Forrester has joined with other economists and engineers at MIT to form a System Dynamics Group, which investigates the effect of technological change on the economy. The group's work also supports the theory of the long wave, but unlike Kondratieff, it offers some empirical data to support the theory. The System Dynamics Group contends that technology leads the economy and that the long wave follows a sudden period of innovation and technological change. The first ascendent portion of the wave results from the implementation of the new technologies within the culture. The last wave started in 1946, after World War II, and was launched by the automobile, chemical, aluminum, communications, and aerospace industries. These industries created secondary booms; in the case of the automobile, for the glass, rubber, machine tool, steel, and plastics industries. The second and descending portion of the long wave is caused by the inability to see that this growth is not endless. Overinvestment in plant capacity results, tying up capital in what ultimately prove to be unnecessary factories and equipment. As demand for the products that led the wave diminishes, factories are shut down, unemployment climbs, and a long period of contraction sets in. This overinvestment also explains the drop in productivity. If capital is invested in an unusable capacity or in the wrong industry altogether, it cannot help but result in declining productivity. At this point, cries are heard for even more investment to boost falling productivity. This is the call for reindustrialization that is popular among politicians today.

If Forrester's theory is correct, then we should see evidence of it in industry. According to Data Resources, Inc., the following industries reached their postwar peak in 1973–74: tires, engines, turbines, farm equipment, glass, textiles, primary iron and steel, electrical transmission equipment, household appliances, process equipment, plastics and synthetics, and nonferrous metals.

By 1978–79, the following industries had also reached their peak level in employment: chemicals, automobiles, trucks, transportation other than cars and trucks, fabricated metal construction supplies, motor vehicle equipment, materials handling, screw machine products, construction equipment, and mining and oilfield equipment. This falloff is not merely hitting the poorly managed industry groups. Well-managed companies such as Boeing, Caterpillar, Phelps-Dodge, and Du Pont have all suffered heavily from the drop in demand for their products.

The putative long waves have been accompanied by three intense periods of financial panic, collapse, and deflation. The first collapse began with the stock market crash in 1826 in Europe and ended with a financial panic in 1837. The second economic collapse occurred in the 1880s and was followed by a long deflationary period. The third was the Great Depression. Each of these periods was preceded by rapid expansion of international lending, resulting in widespread default. In 1826, after a long fall in commodity prices, Spain, Greece, Portugal, and many South American countries defaulted and many merchant banks failed. Following the building up of loans between 1860 and 1872, Spain, Turkey, Egypt, and much of Latin America defaulted, this time on $5 billion in public bonds. Eighteen months before the stock-market crash in 1929, lending began to be restricted as yields from call money and the stock market drew funds away from foreign bonds. During the 1930s over half of the foreign bonds traded in New York and London defaulted, once again because falling commodity prices provided insufficient income to service debt.

Today, there are relatively few foreign bonds traded in New York. Moneys lent to foreign countries come mostly from large banks. If we are in a period of economic contraction, have we placed ourselves in danger of economic collapse as well?

The total owed by developing nations has risen from $72 billion in 1970 to $540 billion at the end of 1981. By the end of 1982 it will have risen to over $600 billion. Over half of the money is owed to commercial banks, the remainder to governments and agencies such as the International Monetary Fund, the Bank for International Settlements, and the World Bank. This generous surge in lending was caused, and in part financed, by the rise in oil prices. Developing nations, strapped for cash and hungry for growth, financed their high oil expenses by borrowing. Much of the money borrowed was petrodollars, oil moneys recycled by OPEC nations through European and American banks. While higher oil prices at first caused inflation in other commodity prices, during the three years since the Iranian-caused oil price hike, worldwide recession has caused demand for commodities to drop. Developing nations depend almost exclusively on their incomes from exported raw material to repay their debts. Whether copper from Chile, phosphate from Morocco, or coffee from Brazil, these are the natural resources and foodstuffs that pay the bill. If developed and developing countries do not buy enough raw materials, prices and demand fall simultaneously, and the debts of developing nations become unserviceable. There were no actual defaults in 1982. No country wants to default and endanger its credit worthiness, so unpayable debts are rescheduled while new loans are arranged. At present 78 percent of Argentina's foreign earnings are required to service its $35 billion foreign debt. For Brazil, 67 percent of its foreign earnings go to paying interest on its $90 billion debt. Mexico's $85 billion debt requires 60 percent. Lending agencies say that no more than 20 percent is prudent. As of fall 1982, thirty-four foreign countries could not meet their payments.

The deterioration of the world's credit system is not merely an issue for sovereign nations. It will have a powerful effect on people throughout the world. By the end of 1982 U.S. banks had loaned $300 billion to the less-developed nations, of which $200 billion went to Latin America. Compare this with the total capital of the ten largest banks in the United States: $40 billion. Five times the capital assets of these banks is at risk in Latin America—for two centuries the most politically and financially volatile continent in the world.

If the world economy should continue to grow and inflate, these debts would pose little short-term threat to the Western creditor banks. But the global economy is both contracting and deflating. The contraction reduces the revenues available to the debtor nations to service their debts while simultaneously reducing world demand for raw materials, causing commodity prices to fall. The banks, instead of acknowledging this dilemma, have used the inability of nations to repay their debts as a means of increasing their profits, in what can only be called the "imagination of growth." Loans that are not repaid are extended—"rolled over"—and interest payments are added to the loan, increasing the total principal owed. At the same time the "spread" on these loans—the rate of interest above the London interbank offered rate, which is tantamount to the international prime rate—is increased. The results, on paper, are higher operating profits for the lending institution.

But will the less-developed nations continue to accept loans that do no more than pay the interest on their outstanding loans and apparently fatten the balance sheets of Western banks, but which in fact do not give the countries any more actual cash to invest in economic growth? When credit was expanding in the 1970s, countries borrowing funds could at least spend the money for whatever economic or political purpose they intended. Now these funds only put them deeper in debt and tie their hands at home as the lenders make the loans on the condition that the borrowers undertake restrictive and unpopular domestic economic policies that conflict with national aims. How long will nations accept this condition?

Richard Russell, the author and publisher of the iconoclastic investment newsletter *Dow Theory Letter*, has been saying for three years that the world must "inflate or die." It is a cold, emphatic statement that flies in the face of the "fine-tuning" notions so characteristic of political economists, who like to think of themselves as engineers. Russell has been joined recently by others who are saying the same thing. In the October 1982 *Forbes*, Norman Gall wrote, "The choice confronting governments everywhere becomes clearer every day: credit contraction or uncontrolled inflation. The politicians will decide." Felix Rohatyn said outright one month later in the *New York Review of Books* that much of $500 billion loaned to developing nations "will never come back" and that there "may be no solution short of a decade of strong, worldwide economic growth."

The credit boom of the 1970s was the world's answer to the abrupt but definitive change in the relationship between labor and energy. One sort of economy, what I call the mass economy, which is based on this critical relationship between declining energy prices and rising wages, has ended without clear identification or acknowledgment that this is so. Instead, nations have borrowed furiously to revive a waning economic structure. The Eurocurrency market has gone from $100 billion in 1970 to nearly $2 trillion today— a credit expansion of floating dollars, yen, francs, and deutsche marks that are largely unregulated by central banks. Mexico, the world's leading debtor nation, has quadrupled its foreign debt since 1975 and increased its internal debt fourteen-fold during the same period. Despite average growth rates in the developed nations of only 2 to 4 percent a year, commercial bank credit has increased during the past decade between 10 and 20 percent in the United States, Japan, Britain, and Germany. As the worldwide recession has taken hold since 1980 and debts have piled up, nations have tried to export themselves into solvency, Brazil being the clearest example. The less-developed nations are trying to restrict imported goods while increasing exports. For many nations, exporting at a loss is better than not exporting at all, since valuable foreign currency can be gained. These exports—steel from Korea, shoes from Brazil—are tearing away at domestic industries in the United States and Europe, raising the specter of protectionism, stiff tariffs, and trade wars to save jobs at home. At the same time, because the less-developed nations are so burdened with debts owed to the West, they no longer represent growing markets for the industrial nations anxious to export capital goods, machinery, and technology. For the first time since the 1974 recession (and, before that, World War II), world trade is contracting. This contraction comes during a period when expansion of trade and economic activity is virtually the only way the world will avoid either a credit collapse leading toward a long period of default and bankruptcy or inflation that soars out of control. If the world cannot pay its debts, the only way to avoid insolvency is to manufacture the money to be repaid. Governments can do this. Either way—credit collapse or inflation—when the dust settles, the world will have less monetary wealth.

Willard Butcher, chairman of Chase Manhattan Bank, contends that it is the lack of economic growth, and not foreign loans, that is responsible for the strain on the banking and economic system. To say that the problem of rising indebtedness and falling international financial liquidity is caused by lack of growth is to overlook the enormous amount of money we have spent for too long in an attempt to replicate the illusion of economic growth. What the economy has been saying since 1973 is that the type of economic growth preceding the oil shock has come to an end and that it must be replaced by a different economy. Thus far, our bankers, financiers, and elected leaders have decided otherwise and have bet the store on future growth. President Reagan has wagered a deficit of three-quarters of a trillion dollars on future growth. The world banking system has over $600 billion at risk in developing countries. Because of this, the world monetary system may collapse.

But the economy will grow, not in the way required or predicted by economic analysts but, rather, in new and surprising ways as the world adapts to the very conditions that bankers, politicians, and businessmen are choosing to ignore: the changing relationship among energy, people, and capital.

❋Chapter 5

The Informative Economy

In every product there is a relationship between the amount of mass and the information that product contains. An ingot of lead has a high ratio of mass to information; a video cassette recorder has a high ratio of information to mass. When we examine a product, it conveys to us something of the knowledge of the producer, through the cut of a garment, the design of a tool, the comfort and solidity of a chair. When we shop, we process large amounts of information about the products we observe. For example, when we buy vegetables and fruits, we check not only for obvious flaws but also note smells, colors, shapes, and other signs that will tell us that the produce is fresh, unblemished, ripe, tasty, and pure. We consider price a critically important part of the complex array of information we sort through. The marketplace is where goods are exchanged, and the mechanism behind this transaction is the exchange of information, through both speech and observation. An item's price is an important part of the information in a product, and it is set between buyer and seller. But most of the information is embodied in the product itself—in its quality, design, utility, and workmanship.

The most basic function of the marketplace is to gather and disseminate information. What we buy, what we will pay, what we demand—this information is fed back into the economy and produces changes in goods and services. But this is not a one-way process. Producers change products that in turn change what we want, demand, and buy. With the exception of rare items such as paintings and precious stones, we value products and services according to how much work (energy) and information has gone into them—shirts are worth more than cotton cloth, cloth is worth more than cotton bales. Generally, the more work put into a product, the higher the price, which points up why the availability and price of energy are so critical to the structure and nature of an economy.

Energy represents potential work. And without work, we have very little. If we can define work as the expenditure of energy to support and sustain life, abundant energy allows us to sustain a high standard of life. Even without abundant energy, a culture that works hard has a higher standard than one that does not. If a culture works hard and has abundant energy, as the United States does, there is, as a result, an extremely high standard of living. But what happens to such a culture when the cost of energy rises so much that it reduces energy's overall usage and availability?

Americans require more work than have the people of any other culture in history. In only six months a U.S. citizen will consume as much energy as a person in a developing nation will in a lifetime. The bulk of that work is done by machines, in factories, through technology. We burn fossil fuels so unthinkingly and in such great quantities that we are impressed by the simplicity of the past. Not long ago, I stood in a park in Stockholm and watched an elderly man make a bee-hive out of a bundle of hay, the kind of dome-shaped hive pictured in fairy tales. A small crowd uttered soft ooohs and aahs as they watched barnyard straw become a useful, strong, and aesthetic object. The man was living history, and we tourists were witnessing a displaced moment in time when most of the useful objects of daily life were made solely by hand without the mediation of machinery or fossil energy.

During the growth of the mass economy, we used continually more energy to run our economy and produce our goods. Thus the amount of energy embodied in products has become a large component of our costs. This has become especially evident as the price of oil has gone up. What has not been so evident is the effect the cost of energy has on the level of information contained within our goods and services. Since using more energy, whether directly or indirectly, makes goods more expensive and therefore less available, we will have to use less energy to produce the same or better goods if we are to maintain our standard of living. To do this, the amount of information per unit of production must increase correspondingly. Remember that we are defining *information* here as design, utility, and durability or, to put it another way, the application of the knowledge of how to best make or accomplish something. The manufacturer must seek ways to make his product a better product, using fewer resources as well as less energy and work. Doing this means finding a better material, redesigning the product, or employing new manufacturing techniques. It may mean using computers to process information, monitor the flow of work, or design components. It may mean using robots to do repetitive mechanical tasks. It may mean changing the way the product is distributed. Whatever methods of improvement are chosen, the goal is the same: to produce more using less. The critical difference between now and twenty years ago is that the manufacturer can no longer just use more energy to increase productivity. It's too expensive. Instead, the manufacturer has to become smarter at what he does.

How does the informative economy use less mass than the mass economy? One way is to make products last longer. Regardless of whether it is a light bulb or a truck, any product designed and manufactured so that its durability is extended is conserving mass.

A second way is to improve quality, which reduces maintenance and operating expenses. Armand V. Feigenbaum, a quality-control consultant, reports that he helped a client redesign a computer printer so that its maintenance costs were reduced from $2,500 to $500 over its useful life. To do this, the price of the printer was increased from $4,000 to $5,000. Not surprisingly, after the change was made, sales of this printer quadrupled.

The third way is to reduce the amount of material in the product. This is being done extensively in the auto and trucking industries. The reduction in size of the American auto was first mandated indirectly by Congress when in 1974 it legislated stringent standards for fuel-efficiency. After 1979 consumers favored smaller, more efficient cars, providing the auto industry with further impetus to change. The simplest way to decrease fuel consumption was to make cars lighter. American automakers have done exactly that, paring away from 1,000 to 2,000 pounds on different models. Using the low figure of 1,000 pounds per car means that in 1982 cars were 5 billion pounds lighter in material than they would have been if they had been made as they were in 1972. In a decade, that equals 250 million tons of iron, steel, aluminum, glass, rubber, plastic, copper, zinc, and lead.

The incentive to reduce material, which industries

call "down-sizing," was provided primarily by expensive energy. Expensive energy, in turn, has made other materials more costly to mine, manufacture, transport, and deliver. As the auto and other industries cut back on the total amount of mass used in manufacturing, this reinforces the decline of the mass economy. Steelworkers are laid off, copper mines are shut down, tire manufacturers close plants, iron ore is not needed. Just as the mass economy was mutually reinforcing—cheaper energy lowered the costs of production, which led to rising wages and increased demand, in turn leading to rising production, resulting in further reduction of product and energy costs—the informative economy rewards the substitution of information for mass by raising the demand for information, which makes information less expensive and thus lowers the cost of goods or at least prevents them from going up in price. This is a new set of rules, and presages an entirely different economy.

In the case of manufactured products, information often takes the form of the semiconductor technology that is transforming product design, function, and cost. Its ubiquitous use saves both material and labor. In cars, sensors in catalytic converters monitor exhaust, relaying information to a microprocessor that can immediately change the air-to-fuel combustion ratio, increasing horsepower and reducing pollution and fuel consumption. Such a system uses far less material than the two- or four-barreled carburetor, but it is material that contains far more information. The semiconductor silicon chip represents a disembodied intelligence that can be applied throughout the economy. Whereas mechanical tools and machines represented the extension of our muscle, today's microelectronics represent the extension of our mind into matter, and their primary economic value will be to reduce the amount of matter consumed. Because we are making mass more intelligent and informed, we will require less to maintain a high standard of living. Because we require less physical stuff, many people whose job it was to make that stuff will be thrown out of work. Millions of people are losing their jobs as the mass economy declines while millions of new jobs are being created as the informative economy emerges. Wealth is being created in the face of suffering, growth alongside economic ruin.

While we are statistically in a recession and have touched the border of a depression, these terms may not be valid. They imply an economic engine running out of steam when in fact we are changing fuels. Not only was energy falling in relative price for one hundred years, but so were steel, transportation, electricity, appliances, textiles, foods, and housing. Now that the decrease in the price of energy has been reversed, so too have the prices of the products that provide us with our standard of living being affected. It is pointless to argue the faults of the present economic structure when we are in the process of discarding it altogether. How can we get the steel and automobile industries back on track when as a nation we have already decided that we want less steel in our cars so that they will get better mileage and be more durable cars, ones worthy of our investing in them?

The raising of oil prices in 1973 prompted the United States to reduce its fuel consumption, and the prolonged economic contraction since 1979 demonstrates the axiom that if one part of the economy is changed, the whole is affected. In saving energy we have cut back on our use of all materials. Cars weigh less, houses are smaller, household appliances have fewer moving parts, and airplanes go further on a gallon of jet fuel.

When the price of goods goes up and incomes remain flat, as they have for the past ten years, people will buy less. They will also buy differently. As incomes shrink, people will search out goods and services that have a higher ratio of information to mass.

With the future growth of income in doubt, the consumer will attempt to buy something that will extend the dollar as far as possible into the future. During the post-World War II period, when goods were falling in price and incomes were rising, there was little incentive to spend so carefully.

One extends one's dollars by buying products that are more informative that is, more durable, better built, more astutely designed, more useful. A 1982 National Science Foundation study of the American automobile industry concluded that if Detroit is to survive foreign competition, it must go through a "cultural revolution"—meaning a radical shift in the attitude of management toward employees, including a change in company policies in order to make people feel involved and committed as well as fundamental changes in the companies' attitude toward the quality of their products. This is precisely the kind of shift in the ratio of mass to information that must occur for any company to survive and prosper in the next economy. In order to put more information into products, companies have to put more information into their employees through education, communication, and honesty.

One of the great myths about economic behavior is that money is the language of the economy. The language of an economy is the information contained in manufacturing, products, and services; money is only a part of that information. If money defined the economy, then anyone with money could open a successful business. But that is not the case. Business success comes from the ability to perceive wants and needs, and that perception depends acutely upon sensitivity to people and their environment.

The problem with the U.S. economy is not the lack of money, material, labor, or industrial capacity. Like so many of the products we manufacture, we suffer instead from a lack of information about who we are, what we are doing, what we want, and how we can proceed from here, given the condition of both the economy and the world we live in. Despite a profoundly shaken economy, products and services that contain a high degree of informativeness are prospering. These include well-made automobiles, clothing, and housewares. Their success has been ascribed to the fact that the rich are unaffected by economic downturns, but I disagree. People of all sorts are changing their purchasing habits. Certainly the rich can do so more easily than others, but that does not change the fact that everyone during the past decade has become more concerned about value, quality, and product life.

The decline in our standard of living may not be a sign of economic failure; rather, it may be part of the cure for our economic ills. It is in the acknowledgment of the slow contraction of our economy that we can create the opportunity to employ ourselves more productively and usefully. The economy may be smarter in its collective activity than we are in our roles as individuals and institutions. At the least, economic contraction arrests our overconsumptive habits.

Like the subway graffito that says "Time is nature's way of preventing everything from happening at once," the period of economic contraction that we have entered may be a way of making sure that we retain sufficient resources and options to change the nature and structure of our economy, resources and options that might be closed off quickly in a period of rapid economic growth.

The informative economy is not a theory. There is not a single manufacturing or service industry that does not reflect the shift to it from the mass economy. The informative economy describes how we are responding—or not responding—to new economic realities. We are buying more foreign cars not because they are foreign but because they have been more intelligently designed, more carefully put together, and are more economical to run. The underlying difference between a Chevette and a Honda is information, not mass. Each has roughly the same amount of plastic, rubber, chrome, and steel, but one is superior in design, craftsmanship, and performance. This is not to lionize the Japanese; it is to point out the intelligence of the U.S. consumer. Not only are Americans choosing Hondas over Chevettes but they are keeping them longer than they kept cars in the past. Americans are increasingly willing to pay more for something that lasts longer, which means each of us can be expected to buy fewer cars over a lifetime than would have been projected ten years ago. If in 1981 General Motors produces the equivalent of a 1973 Toyota and wonders why it is losing market share to the Japanese, it is not because of an eight-year difference in steel, chrome, or rubber but an eight-year gap in information and intelligence. Nor is the information privileged, secret, or available only to the powerful or wealthy; it is available everywhere, from the news, and, particularly, from perceiving how we lead our lives. The information comes from a decade during which we have faced lowered incomes and enormous leaps in the prices of energy, food, public services, and real estate, and increasing economic uncertainty.

What the informative economy recognizes and encourages is that it is labor and management, not merely capital or energy, that bring worth to mass. However, it is not labor and management per se but intelligent labor and intelligent management that imbue mass with a higher quality or nature. In the mass economy, differences among workers in labor, skill, and ability were leveled by the long production runs required to attain "economies of scale." It did not matter how skillful a welder was if the assembly line was set up for average welding skills. The need for products that are better built will require that higher skills be developed and deployed, and this will necessitate a change in the assembly and production techniques practiced by many manufacturers—the "cultural revolution" referred to by the National Science Foundation.

In the mass economy, labor went up in value while the goods that labor could buy often went down not only in price, but in quality, durability, and workmanship. To change this means that more informed labor will go into each product. In classical economics this would signify that productivity has gone down; informative economics would say that the amount of information in each product has gone up. This suggests the simple notion that mass diminishes intelligence, whereas intelligence enhances mass. In other words, when we are saturated with goods, there is little motivation to inform those goods with intelligence. But when the amount of goods we can have is reduced, there is every incentive to become more intelligent about their creation, selection, use, and care.

A characteristic of the mass economy was the concept that more was better or, in the case of goods, that having mass-produced goods was better for everyone than higher-quality, labor-intensive goods. As long as resources were seemingly unlimited and inexpensive, mass production gave people more goods. That these goods wore out easily or became less useful within a shorter time did not matter because the replacement cost of goods was usually lower than the original purchase price. We are often shown figures illustrating how many fewer hours of work it takes an American to buy a car or a refrigerator than a Russian or a Brazilian. By those standards the United States is clearly well off. But we have reached a point where the advantage achieved by making the greatest number of goods is negated by the loss of their quality.

In an informative economy, we change from an affluent to an *influent* society. If you are affluent, goods and services flow toward you; if you are influent, the information contained within goods flows into you. An affluent society may possess an opulent and abundant amount of goods, but that does not mean it will be able to utilize, appreciate, and maintain them. An influent society will have less, but its relationship to what it has will be more involved and concerned; people will take care of what they have, and what they have will mean more to them. In other words, an affluent society amasses goods, while an influent society processes the information within goods.

Los Angeles is an affluent city, sprawling over 4,000 square miles of canyons, basins, hills, and coasts. One-third of its total land area is occupied by roads and parking lots, a design that seemed, if not sensible, at least permissible when gasoline was cheap and the automobile king. Because it grew in a time of cheap energy, Los Angeles is designed for and around the car. The city requires a high level of road maintenance, makes necessary high fuel use per capita, generates a substantial amount of waste, and has almost no neighborhoods.

Village Homes, built and developed by Michael Corbett in Davis, California, after the first energy crisis in 1973, is an influent community. It was designed with streets half the conventional width, with most ending as cul-de-sacs to prevent through-traffic. The homes, which are solar-heated, are built in clusters. The 70-acre, 235-unit development gives up only one-tenth of its space to roads, and residents use only one-tenth to one-half the energy of Los Angelenos. The sense of community growing out of the development has meant a lower crime rate than that in Los Angeles or even in surrounding neighborhoods, as well as more interaction among residents, local production of food, and less reliance on outside resources and services than in a city like Los Angeles.

The informative economy requires more intelligence from everyone—management, labor, consumers, governments. Those who do not become learners again, regardless of age or rank, will find themselves at an increasing disadvantage as the informative economy takes root. Japan is the best example of a society that takes this precept firmly to heart. One of the most impressive characteristics of the Japanese is their ability to learn new things. They are inveterate probers and questioners and approach everything with an attitude of curiosity. Unlike our educational system, which places high value on innovation and individuality, the Japanese method of learning is to find that which is paramount in a field and imitate it perfectly. By examining what has been exemplary in the recent past in all its aspects and minutiae, the Japanese prepare themselves for later innovation. This method of analysis and imitation has enabled them to establish international dominance in industry after industry. They have defined the purpose of business management as not only administration but also the gathering and dissemination of information. In contrast to U.S. corporate management, the Japanese, although personally as conservative as their U.S. counterparts, seem much more accepting of change and new ideas. After Japan's disastrous attempts to seize a resource base by military means in World War I and World War II, it concluded that its survival depended on intelligence rather than muscle. Since World War II, Japan has spent $10 billion in licensing fees and royalties to obtain technologies and patents that would enable it to avoid reinventing the wheel. By absorbing as much as possible about technologies created by others, Japan has been able to build its research base on what was already accomplished elsewhere.

The role of the government in the mass economy has been to keep the economic kettle boiling, primarily through monetary and tax policies. U.S. government, like big business, has defined its role as the gatherer and keeper of information rather than the distributor of that information to society. One of the enormous vanities of being at the locus of incoming information is to think that one is consequently best qualified to act on it. There is no better example of this than Washington's response to the rise of oil prices in 1973. At that time there was federal regulation of oil and natural gas prices. Because of political pressure, President Nixon did not try to lift controls on oil. When Ford succeeded Nixon, he requested that Congress deregulate the prices of both natural gas and oil in order to encourage conservation. Ford also proposed a $3-per-barrel tariff on imported oil to further discourage its consumption. But the Democratic-controlled Congress had different ideas and instead lowered the maximum selling price of domestic oil by 15 percent. So while the rest of the world was paying over $15 a barrel, the United States was paying closer to $8 for its domestic oil.

The retention of price controls was supposed to protect U.S. consumers from high prices; instead, consumers were fooled. The price of a commodity in the marketplace is important information. By controlling prices (information), the government was in effect spreading disinformation throughout the economy. The American people, once the recessionary shock of OPEC's price hikes wore off in 1975, returned to buying big cars and burning vast amounts of motor fuel. Thus the government was rewarding consumptive behavior when consumers should have been conserving and learning to adapt to an era of expensive energy. Similarly, energy-intensive businesses were not provided with sufficient incentives to invest in more energy-efficient and productive machinery and technology. One result was the near-bankruptcy of Chrysler, burdened by the fact that its customers continued to demand large cars through the seventies and also that it was making its cars in antiquated and inefficient factories. When the price of oil climbed again after the Iranian revolution in 1979, big cars became a glut on the market and Chrysler initially could not compete with the Japanese in the efficient production of small, high-mileage cars. Between 1978 and 1981 Chrysler's market share dropped from 12.3 percent to 7.1 percent, displacing forty thousand workers from their jobs.

Japan, like the United States, was also hit by increases in energy prices in 1973–74. Because it imports all of its oil, Japan had no insulation from price increases and it suffered a severe recession known there as the "oil shokku." Because it had no alternatives, Japan had to apply its resources to adaptation quickly. Its heavy industries, including steel, shipbuilding, and automobiles, did not retreat but instead invested tens of billions of dollars to make their manufacturing processes more efficient. By 1976 Japan had emerged from its most severe postwar recession in a powerfully competitive position, running up an export surplus of $50 billion in the next three years, a time when the United States was incurring $90 billion in trade deficits largely because of oil importation.

The critically important difference between the two countries was the dissemination of information. In Japan, the new price of oil was accepted and immediately acted upon by the nation. In the United States, price rises were suppressed and the question of energy was so politicized that by 1979 most Americans still thought that there was no fundamental energy problem. By concentrating on the politically inspired question as to whether there was a "real" energy shortage, Americans overlooked the most important point: the real cost of energy was climbing higher and higher.

It appears that U.S. candidates view politics as a game of obfuscation, as demonstrated by their uncertainty about how much information should be allowed to enter the political dialogue. Candidates for President in 1980 should have told the American people that the economy was so laden with past excesses and political conveniences that whoever gained power would preside over an economic mess for at least four years. Ronald Reagan promised a balanced budget but found instead that he would create in four and a half years some $700 to $800 billion in deficits—an amount equal to the total federal deficit for the first two hundred years of the republic. By devising fiscal and tax policies that are oriented toward re-creating old growth curves in old industries, we are failing to learn the lesson that Japan gained immediately after the first oil shock: adaptation.

One of the correct pieces of information the government gave out in 1981 is that in 1980 wages dropped more than at any time since the Great Depression. If the new ratio of values among labor, capital, and energy is sustained, then this wage decline will continue for many years. The prospect of continually lower wages is not appealing, but unless we understand the mechanism whereby wages are falling and will continue to fall, it will be difficult to adapt our economic behavior to meet and compensate for the decline. As long as the industrialized world was successful in transferring work from human energy to fossil energy, the ability of one person to produce more goods increased. Increased productivity permitted higher wages and cheaper goods. Capital was readily available at reasonable cost and our gross national product rose. Society prospered as long as increases in production exceeded increases in the cost of the fossil-fuel energy that was substituted for the work of human energy.

The sudden reversal of the downward trend in oil prices has had a direct effect on the value of labor in the United States, as shown in Table 8. In the first column are the average weekly wages in current dollars of a full-time employee covering the years from 1900 to 1982. In the next column are the same wages expressed with inflation factored out in constant 1967 dollars. In the third column are the prices of oil in 1967 constant dollars. The last column shows how many hours an average employee had to work in order to buy a barrel of oil. Starting in 1900, a person had to work 4.8 hours in order to buy one barrel of oil. In the years following, the required amount of labor for oil dropped steadily until the period between 1970 and 1973, during which a barrel of oil required only 36 minutes of labor. Not surprisingly, this coincides with the period when the purchasing power of Americans was at its highest and when production, factory utilization, and many other economic indices showed the U.S. economy at its peak. Notice, too, in Column 2, that wages hit their peak in 1973 and have been falling since. By 1982 wages had fallen 16 percent and the time required to purchase a barrel of oil had increased 6.5 times to 3.9 hours, higher than it was in 1910.

The purpose of Table 8 is to illustrate one of the main contentions of this book: that the ratio of values between labor and energy is changing. The economy is more like a dance than a statistical table, and movement is the key to understanding it. The movement illustrated in this table is not something that will soon be reversed. In just one decade, we have returned to the historical relationships regarding values with which we began the century.

The United States uses the energy equivalent of about 32 million barrels of oil a day. Twenty-four percent is used by industry (approximately 8 million barrels of oil a day). While there are over 100 million people employed in this country, much of the actual *work* on a given day is accomplished by the energy equivalent of those 8 million barrels rather than those workers. "Work" means the activity that produces food, clothing, warmth, shelter, and all basic human needs. When energy costs quadruple, as they did in 1973, our work costs more and what we produce costs more. In 1973 something had to give, and in the case of industrialized nations, what gave were prices, which rose, and wage increases, which lagged—a combination that was tantamount to real cuts in pay.

It is important to understand that the present relationship among labor, capital, and energy has nothing to do with whether we import oil or whether we are energy independent. There are predictions that by 1996

Table 8*

	Weekly Wages (current)	Weekly Wages (constant)	Cost/Barrel (constant)	Hours/Barrel
1900	8	32	3.80	4.8
1910	11	41	2.55	2.5
1920	26	57	4.42	3.1
1930	27	54	2.62	1.9
1940	25	60	2.59	1.7
1950	58	81	3.23	1.6
1960	93	106	3.45	1.3
1970	148	128	1.79	0.6
1971	158	131	1.91	0.6
1972	168	134	1.85	0.6
1973	179	135	1.95	0.6
1974	192	130	7.92	2.4
1975	208	129	7.14	2.2
1976	223	131	6.77	2.1
1977	238	131	6.85	2.1
1978	256	131	6.51	2.0
1979	277	127	7.82	2.5
1980	302	120	12.75	4.3
1981	316	116	12.47	4.3
1982 (prelim.)	330	113	10.94	3.9

* Adapted from *Survey of Current Business: The National Income and Product Accounts of the United States, 1929–74*, U.S. Department of Commerce, Bureau of Economic Analysis, 1981; Statistical Abstract No. 342, 1970; Rees, Albert, *Real Wages in Manufacturing, 1890 to 1914*, New York: National Bureau of Economic Research, 1961; *Handbook of Labor Statistics 1975*—reference ed., U.S. Department of Labor; *Statistical Abstract* No. 792, 1980; Statistical Abstract No. 676, 1981.

the United States will be 90 percent self-sufficient in energy, but the rosiness of such forecasts should not obscure self-sufficiency's price. While the United States will be stronger economically when it relies less on volatile sources and supply lines for its energy, we should not assume that this energy will be cheap; the cost of energy will continue to rise because it takes more and more work to produce a given amount of energy. (While this may not be true in Saudi Arabia, world oil prices reflect this fact.) And as more work goes into producing energy, less work is available to produce goods and services, which means the price of goods will rise.

The ability to produce products with a higher ratio of information to mass is more easily accomplished by small businesses than large ones because small businesses can change more quickly, have better internal communication, and can tailor their products more specifically to smaller markets. But that does not mean large companies cannot produce highly informative goods. The Japanese (as well as IBM) have proven they can produce informative goods on a large scale. That Japanese businesses can create such products on a large scale means that they are developing intelligent management systems. Such systems would be of no use to the Japanese if their goal was to make products that were merely cheaper than U.S. ones. Their aim is to make products with greater utility and performance while using less material (mass). This is not an exclusively Japanese business characteristic, but the Japanese, with their tradition of having a few carefully made possessions, have made an accurate reading of where the world must go as we approach the twenty-first century.

One of the reasons U.S. business is slow to grasp the kind of changes necessary to make the shift from a mass to an informative economy is that no one can buy what is needed to make the transition. The mass economy can be broken down into components, most of which can be quantified in dollars, including its people and managers. To make a company more intelligent, to bring a work force together, to create and design better products, to eliminate waste, and to constantly receive innovative techniques and ideas from employees—these are elements that cannot be purchased like new plants, machines, or licenses. These changes are not forbidden to big business, but they are more difficult to achieve in a large company that does not already strive for these qualities than in a smaller and newer company. Chrysler originally had more money than Honda, but Honda apparently had a better idea about the future.

❋ Chapter 6

Growth or
Change?

There is no better example of the shift from a mass to an informative economy than energy conservation. To conserve means to reduce the amount of mass—in this case, energy, in the form of oil, coal, and gas—used by industry, transportation, and housing. To do so requires information—new technologies, improved designs, and better maintenance. Pacific Gas and Electric, the nation's largest utility, has realized that it is less expensive for them to offer no-interest loans to homeowners for insulation and weatherstripping than it is to borrow capital and build new power plants. By applying new ideas and techniques in an effort to decrease existing energy consumption, the economy can produce as much as it had formerly, reducing costs and lowering the ratio of mass to information. The Mellon Institute estimates that the United States can reduce the amount of energy used in producing a GNP dollar from the 55,000 Btus required in 1973 to 27,000 Btus by the year 2000.

It was a reflection of the philosophy of the mass economy that conservation was considered a negligible factor in the ability of the United States to achieve energy independence. All administrations since 1973 have concentrated on *new* energy production. President Reagan, asked about conservation in his energy policy, defined it as "being hot in the summer and cold in the winter." Despite such government attitudes, the U.S. economy is moving rapidly toward energy conservation, promising to make it one of the biggest industries of the informative economy. It is estimated that by 1990 the energy conservation industry could total between $50 billion and $70 billion. Other major areas would be co-generation systems, where steam wasted in generating electricity would be recaptured to produce heat; more efficient electric motors that could save the United States 10 percent of all the electricity it consumes; energy management systems in large and small buildings; and industrial heat recovery. Further, the U.S. auto industry will be producing cars whose fleet mileage will average 40 miles per gallon—almost triple the 1974 average of 14 miles per gallon.

Reagan's attitudes reflect the commonly held belief that energy conservation is not economic growth whereas energy exploration and development are. If our view of healthy economic growth is synonymous with more, what do we call an economy that consumes less and preserves more? For example, suppose a person who used to buy a new car every three years finds a mechanic who makes this proposition: he will maintain the new car from the outset for a period of twelve years for a flat fee of $1,000 per year plus parts. The contract, although expensive at first, as times goes on, shifts the advantage to the owner, who has not had to replace his vehicle in the fourth, seventh, and tenth years. The mechanic will only benefit if he does an excellent job of maintenance. If he does a bad job, the car will break down, and his income per hour will drop. In this situation, society has received the benefit of a car—transportation—for less cost than it would have if it had replaced the car; less materials have been used and more labor has been used per year than would have been employed making a new car every three years. The problem is that productivity has gone down and the economy has shrunk, as has the auto industry. Such a practice would be reminiscent of the ancient Chinese method of paying the physician a retainer as long as the patient is healthy; when the patient gets sick, the retainer is dropped until the patient recovers. The incentive on the doctor's side is to keep the patient healthy, as no benefit is derived from pathology. Since the GNP currently grows as someone gets ill, is an economy in which the GNP goes up when cars last and people are healthy conceivable? Imagining such an economy requires an entirely different comprehension of growth.

Just what is growing in our economy? Do we necessarily want *all* that grows? If we use fewer drugs or X rays or spare parts in our bodies, are we a failing economy? We do not bemoan the fact that when our sons and daughters come of age they cease to grow taller. At adulthood, we entirely redefine the concept of growth. Can we not define an economy similarly? The "unremitting cultivation of goods," as George Gilder, author of *Wealth and Poverty*, describes a capitalist economy, is but mere incessancy. We now require a new definition of growth—a type of growth that will allow us to use our resources more conservatively. If you make an economy expand, it has grown. If you take what is grown and make it more complex, self-aware, accurate, and effective but do not expand its boundaries or external scope, it has *internally differentiated*. What exists has become more refined—more specific to task, function, and need. This requires labor, materials, energy, capital, communication, and virtually all the other components that go into an economy, but the proportion of the components used is altered.

The informative economy will not replace the mass economy; it will absorb and include the mass economy in the course of its evolution. We will need steel, rubber, airplanes, pulp mills, and trucks for centuries. The industrial age was not a failure but an unmitigated success. If we refuse to change and try to extend the industrial age beyond its useful life, we will change success into failure by not recognizing our maturation.

The shift of the mass economy to the informative economy can be compared with "product life-cycle" theory. When a successful product is introduced, demand for it grows quickly and emphasis is placed on the rate of production. As demand begins to be satisfied, variations of the new product are introduced. Again, economic emphasis is on the rate of production to satisfy demand. Eventually the market approaches saturation and resources that were formerly directed toward increasing the rate of production are channeled into improving the quality of the product—in production, performance, and cost. While this phenomenon has long been observed in certain product cycles, the theory has not been applied to the macroeconomy as a whole.

In the case of the economy, the underlying reasons for the shift from mass to information are different from those leading to an improved product. In product life-cycle theory, the shift in emphasis from the rate of production to the quality of production is caused by a decline in demand. The shift from the mass economy to the informative economy is being caused by the decline in the availability of inexpensive energy. In other words, it is being caused by a decline in the supply of resources rather than a decline in the demand for goods. In this respect, the economy during its present period of transition resembles a species adapting to a changing environment.

The mass economy carried with it a sense of unlimited horizons and resources that was confirmed by the falling prices of most raw materials since 1870. That resources in fact are limited is not important, because the economy, if we may ascribe animatedness to it, has acted as though resources were unlimited. Because of this, the one-hundred-year period between 1870 and 1970 was dominated by a high rate of growth and replication. There was no attention given to the maximum carrying capacity of the environment with respect to economic activity because very few obstacles to growth were perceived. This sort of activity is referred to as asymptotic growth and can be symbolized on a chart by a J curve, because it starts out as a curving line and eventually becomes closer to a straight line of growth perpendicular to the base of a chart or graph. In nature, when J-curve growth (see Figure 1, page 95) occurs among fauna, such growth is rewarded with a "bust" because species growth soon outstrips the environment's food supply. At that point, population growth halts and contracts to a point where the environment can support this new lower level of population. This pattern of boom and bust applies whether we are talking about starfish on a reef or deer in a forest.

There is another type of adaptation to rapid population growth seen in nature, and this is represented by a sigmoid, or S, curve. In both J and S growth, the population, whether birds, bushes, or bacteria, expands as much as the supply of food or nutrients allows. Since there seem to be no limits at first, growth starts as an exponential curve, but in S-curve growth the species begins to detect limits to population expansion.

These limits are the capacity of the environment

to provide food at the same rate as the rate of population expansion. In S-curve growth, feedback results that causes the species to limit the rate of reproduction, producing the reversal from an exponential curve to a sigmoid curve. What is often observed is not a smooth, perfect S, but the beginning of an S curve followed by rapid oscillations of growth and contraction, amounting to no overall growth. A species long accustomed to growth cannot immediately adjust its rate of reproduction to the end-capacity of the environment.

Using growth curves seen in animal population expansion as an analogy for economic behavior, we can see in Figure 1 that the informative economy is not different from the mass economy, but, rather, that it describes a more mature stage of economic development, a stage that at first will be volatile, turbulent, and chaotic. As I have drawn the chart representing the economy, my guess is that we are on the point marked with an X. We have experienced nine gross years of slow growth—a tapering off of the rate of expansion of our gross national product. And what we are now seeing, in the policies prescribed by President Reagan and his economic advisers, and in the rapid rise in the stock market, is an institutional attempt to replicate old rates of growth experienced earlier on the chart. This can only be sustained for very short periods of time, and the more intensely we attempt to re-create old patterns of growth, the sharper the correction as shown on the chart will be. In other words, we are attempting a mini J curve as we reach the peak of culmination of the S curve. And it could result in a bust.

What becomes obvious when one uses such a chart to depict economic transition is that strategies appropriate during the rapid growth of the mass economy are inappropriate to its mature phase, the informative economy. Although some of the mass economic strategies and qualities have been discussed in previous chapters, they are worth repeating here as a group in order to contrast them with strategies appropriate to the informative economy.

As the mass economy moves toward the informative economy, there will initially be disorder, because the activity of all economic components must change behavior, movement, and pattern. Products must change. Energy-intensity, marketing, consumption, and consumer habits must also change. Each component of the mass economy must either adapt or perish, but it will take time to understand what part each plays (or no longer plays) in what will be the new economy. This

Figure 1

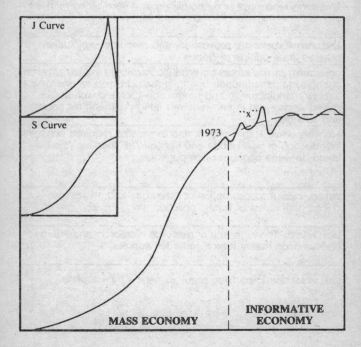

Qualities and

MASS ECONOMY

EXPANSIVE: Everything grew in scale. An idea became a shop, a shop became a chain, a chain became an industry — for example, McDonald's. Cheaper resources favored centralized manufacturing and therefore large-scale factories' distribution and marketing. Expansion was a rising sea that lifted much before it but left many smaller businesses submerged.

REPLICATIVE: Large-scale production required product uniformity and long runs to achieve maximum efficiency. Styles were homogenized, the United States became a poor copy of itself.

ACCRETIVE: Wealth and power were achieved by gathering and amassing resources or by cornering and dominating markets.

AFFLUENT: Expansion, replication, and resource exploitation created large outflow of goods.

CONSUMPTIVE: The stress on production prior to industrialization changed to consumption during industrialization as energy-intensive manufacturing and production-liberated workers raised wages and in turn required a high demand for goods and services.

INTERMEDIATIVE: Rapid growth and expansion required constant introduction of new goods and services to "mediate" the distance between economic components.

ENTROPIC: High consumption of resources and energy produced high levels of waste, pollution, annd toxicity.

HIGH WAGES: The high rate of resource extraction and energy consumption meant high income for workers.

SPECIALIZATION: Expansion required narrow sets of skills.

Strategies

INFORMATIVE ECONOMY

CONTRACTIVE: In an environment of unlimited resources, expansion is the key to survival in business. When resources are no longer limitless or inexpensive, contraction can be the key to survival. Witness how many corporations have divested assets, subsidiaries, and property. Contraction makes consumers smarter and business leaner.

DIFFERENTIATIVE: Contraction causes mass markets to break up. Production must become more flexible to meet specific needs of smaller groups. Production efficiency is not as important as consumption utility: "Does the product really work for me?"

MUTUAL: Instead of accretion, society benefits from mutuality of interests in order to maintain living standards. Adversary regulation and rule are too expensive; power accrues to those who can bring groups together.

INFLUENT: Fewer overall goods means benefits of goods are achieved by widespread use rather than single ownership.

CONSERVATIVE: Overconsumptive ethic threatens well-being of society because it reduces what is available for all, thus causes shift to conservative ethic.

DISINTERMEDIATIVE: Contraction and increasing population stability will mean less need for intermediaries; will instead promote "disintermediation" (discussed in Chapter 8): more efficient economic pathways created to conserve energy, resources, and unnecessary labor.

INFORMATION-RICH: Instead of excess of expended resources causing entropic decay, there can be excess of information causing overload and stress to systems.

LOWER WAGES: Resource consumption is conserved by the substitution of people for energy; wages slowly fall and stabilize at a new level.

BROAD SKILLS: In mass economy, rewards were for specialization and consumption. In informative society, people need to have general skills, be more self-sufficient (disintermediative) and less reliant on specialists. Higher ratio of information to mass demands more knowledge by each participant in management and business.

loosening, or untightening of the economy, is a necessary stage in the creation of another system. The new informative system will be characterized in part by the merging of the old science of economics with the newer science of ecology. Economic laws, theories, and observations such as Gresham's Law and the theory of the marginal efficiency of capital are still valid, but they must be applied to a new context.

Ecology is the study of the relationship between organisms and their environments. Since our wealth, economic health, and real growth now depend intimately on our understanding of our environment, any business or economist without an ecological sensitivity runs the risk of not adapting. For decades, ecological science could be ignored by businesses and economists because the environment was forgiving of demands placed on it. The earth was large enough and the population small enough to allow us to ignore the limits of resources and the expense of waste. Now we must pay attention to what the environment tells us.

Gently but firmly, the environment is telling us that we are outstripping its capacity to fill our current demands. According to Lester Brown, author of *Building a Sustainable Society*, the world reached a major watershed in 1960 that we have yet to acknowledge. That year world population reached 3 billion, and for the first time "the yields of the three basic biological systems [forests, seas, and grasslands] expanded less rapidly than population." Since that time, the margin between total demand and total output has narrowed and even become negative, so that today we are eating into past reserves. Many items, such as fish, wool, and meat, have steadily dropped in both per capita and absolute production since the early 1970s. Part of this biological shortfall was met by such intensive use of petroleum-based fertilizers and mechanization that fertilizer usage increased 600 percent between 1950 and 1980. During that time, population and production did *not* increase 600 percent. This means that reliance on oil increased faster than the rate of population growth and the increase in basic foodstuffs. There is no end in sight to this disproportionate growth.

The mass economy has met food demand through the industrialization of agriculture. Large equipment operating on large farms has changed farming from labor intensive to capital and energy intensive. The problem with increased U.S. food production has been that intensive methods of cultivation and fertilization are rapidly reducing the amount of topsoil and topsoil fertility. In other words, we have turned our farms into mines, and what we are extracting with our food is long-term fertility or, at the very least, the ability of the land to produce food without increasingly expensive applications of fertilizers and pesticides.

The industrialization of agriculture was made possible by the low cost of energy. We could afford to use more energy per unit of output, reducing our labor costs during a period when labor was leaving the farm for higher-paying jobs. It is estimated that the United States expends 10 calories for every calorie of food taken off the field, while the Chinese spend 1. China, in order to achieve yields at one-tenth the energy cost of ours, uses more labor. While the United States does not want to go back to a labor-intensive agriculture to save energy, U.S. farmers are faced with the prospect of continually higher operating costs and dwindling profits. However, the world is making more people, not more land. Our only hope of supplying sufficient amounts of food for ourselves and others is to have more people on the land working ever more productively.

Having more people work the land flies in the face of conventional wisdom about the benefits of increasing mechanization but conforms closely to the idea of an informative economy. For food production to increase and the land to regain its fertility, there will have to be a shift in the ratio of mass to information. Mass is represented by land and energy; information by intelligence, technique, and people. Smaller, more intensively worked farms are considered a romantic notion. It was Secretary of Agriculture Earl Butz, under President Nixon, who advised American farmers to "get big or get out." But during the past three years, many of the farmers who got big got out, bankrupted by the high cost of capital, while conservative farmers who stayed small and kept their debts low survived. More important, the cost of oil in the form of diesel fuel, pesticides, herbicides, and nitrogenous fertilizers has skyrocketed since 1973. With the ongoing decontrol of natural gas, which is the main component of anhydrous ammonia, the cost of fertilizers is expected to triple within the next five years.

What made American farmers the most productive in the world is now threatening to put them out of business: abundant energy. From a labor-intensive livelihood, farming has become a capital- and energy-intensive industry that requires the investment of large amounts of capital and energy into the land and obtains high yields in return. But like big industry, farmers have been fooled. By putting so much capital into energy-intensive machinery and technologies, they are being driven into insolvency. In 1982 farmers earned $19 billion in income—about the same amount as they did in 1932 when the earlier figure is adjusted for inflation. But this income will not even service their $200 billion in land, equipment, and farm debt. Land prices have skyrocketed since World War II, primarily because such large yields could be obtained. New farmers who try to start out by purchasing their own land are locked into trying to obtain the very highest yields in order to make their land payments. This means intensive cultivation and fertilization. Because farmers have been successful in producing fence-to-fence, there is too much food, which has resulted in depressed crop prices. These conditions in turn have forced farmers to try to produce themselves out of their financial difficulties. Thus, in 1982, we had record yields of wheat, corn, and soybeans—and the greatest number of farm bankruptcies since the Depression.

The shift from a mass to an informative economy reverses the polarities of what is and isn't economical. It *was* romantic to think of farming a small amount of land in the past few decades, because the economies of scale prevented a person from making a living unless he was growing specialty crops like wine grapes or tobacco. The $50,000 combine and $40,000 tractor didn't pay for themselves on the 100-acre farm. And for many years small equipment didn't pay either as land prices rose and crop prices fell. Equally romantic now may be the large farm, or, at the very least, starting a large farm and having it service its debt or give even a moderate return on equity. Whether the farm is large or small, the means to make a farm pay for itself are the same. The farm must produce more income relative to expenses. Since U.S. farms, in general, have pushed yields to the upper limits of the soil's capacity, the answer must involve lowering costs. And the way one lowers the cost of fertilizers, equipment, fuel, pesticides, and herbicides is to use less or to use them not at all. So-called biological farming techniques, once considered frivolous or idealistic, were recommended for serious consideration by Bob Bergland, secretary of agriculture during the Carter administration. Bergland said that organic farming could rebuild soil fertility while lowering the costs of production. The way to farm with a minimum of fossil fuels and chemicals is to farm smarter: to know the land, the crops, the pests, and the cycles, and to develop a farming technique that uses nature instead of fighting it. That kind of knowledge cannot be applied mechanically; it must be derived from experience.

As long as farmers could replace labor with machinery and fertility with fertilizers, the green revolution could proceed apace. Farming could make the huge productivity gains it has during the past fifty years. With the peaking of the mass economy, much of what the farmer learned is no longer useful in adapting to a time of rising resource prices. The knowledge that is required now is not how to wring more out of the soil but how to obtain suitable yields with *less*. If you are using pesticides, you want to know what will kill aphids or whitefly. If you wish to eliminate pesticide expenses, you have to know how to attract ladybugs. Learning to use fewer resources per acre will require large farms either to add more trained personnel or to begin a gradual reduction in farm size in order to be worked intelligently. Farms will slowly become smaller because it will be easier for a smaller farmer to make money than a giant farmer. And as this happens, a vast new field of agricultural technology will open up.

In countries where geography or demographics prohibit large holdings, there is already a demand for such technology. In the United States, the need for downsized machinery will be slow in building, since land ownership patterns can only change gradually over decades. Nevertheless, American companies are feeling the impact of this changing demand, particularly in their export sales. While International Harvester staggers toward a possible bankruptcy, Kubota of Japan is flourishing overseas and in the U.S. market. Kubota has aggressively pursued the small and intermediate-size tractor business, a market American manufacturers largely ignored while concentrating on air-conditioned, cab-over rigs equipped with televisions, lasers, and telephones.

The conclusion that small farms work better than large farms has recently been confirmed by the Department of Agriculture. In a 1981 study, it found that in the corn belt the most efficient farms were those of

640 acres, but that over 90 percent efficiency could be attained by farms of 300 acres. On wheat farms, the most efficient were found to be ones with 1,476 acres, but again, 90 percent efficiency could be accomplished on 232-acre farms. By contrast, in some developing countries, the most efficient farms have between 1 and 5 acres. In both cases, the most efficient farm size is one that can be worked by a family who owns their land, or at least receives the fruits of their work and production. Whereas the U.S. farmer can afford the machinery to work 640 acres, the farmer in India must cultivate largely by hand. Each case reflects a different ratio of mass to information, but a proper one for the land and economy in question.

There is also a social ecology to adhere to in an informative economy. This is the way people relate to their greater environment, what philosopher James Ogilvy refers to as our "neo-nature," the human-made environment around us comprised of cities, institutions, employers, neighborhoods, and laws. Our relationship to that environment must also change. For example, as the economy begins to contract, there already has been a market change in the relationship between unions and business. During the expansionary stages of the mass economy, growth required a "who gets what?" bargaining strategy. Unions and big business were fighting over the spoils by using each other's withdrawal from participation—strikes or lockouts—as bargaining chips. Now that real contraction has set in, both business and unions recognize that their survival depends on the other. Recent union settlements, for the most part, have been characterized by a "who gives what?" approach, one where each side is making concessions to the other in order to get what both need: jobs, profits, and survival.

For example, Uniroyal has created a council composed of workers and management that will engage in an ongoing discussion of the company's finances, marketing, and corporate planning. Unions also have been granted the right to make presentations to Uniroyal's board of directors, in return for which they gave up cost-of-living allowances for three years, which would have increased salaries by $25 million.

Timken, the ball-bearing manufacturer, has agreed not to relocate to a new plant in the Sunbelt, in exchange for an eleven-year no-strike clause in the new union contract. Colt Industries, McLouth Steel, Pan American Airways, Continental, United Airlines, and Western Airlines have agreed to open their books to unions in return for pay freezes or cuts.

To cope with rapid economic change and the need for workers and management alike to keep abreast of new developments, Japanese management rotates their employees through different jobs, avoiding the overspecialization so common to U.S. business. The advantages of rotating personnel through a corporation are threefold: one, a worker does not solely identify with one part of the company but sees himself or herself as part of an integrated whole; second, crossfertilization of staff develops better channels of communication among departments, eliminating battles over turf; third, people who feel they can move through and about an organization will be more likely to stay with that company, which eliminates costly turnover while building employee experience, flexibility, and loyalty. Rotating people so that they accumulate generalist skills rather than specialist skills provides them with a sense of learning and development and maintains for them an atmosphere of being in an information-rich environment where one is constantly challenged by new ideas.

For an informative economy to succeed, we must inform each other about what we do and how we work. In a booming and expansive economy, there may be complex interrelationships between individuals as entities in an economy, but there is no real dependence because economic growth provides an abundance of new wealth. When an economy stabilizes or contracts, our individual condition and standard of living comes to rely much more heavily on the actions and decisions of others. This is the kind of behavior seen in a flood or natural disaster: hardship brings all together under a common purpose that supersedes the petty differences that may have formerly existed. We are not undergoing economic disaster, but instead are experiencing a slow but inexorable change in our national wealth, a shift from mass to information. To be informed is to learn. It is no accident that the world's leading technology company, IBM, spends $500 million per year in training, educating, and reeducating its employees. In the informative economy, learning will be essential for all healthy economic activity. This learning results from paying attention to the feedback provided by the environment to the economy. By ignoring it we risk a bust, both personally and nationally. By paying attention, we can adapt.

❃ Chapter 7

Some Informative Strategies

The informative economy infuses economic activity with new techniques, knowledge, and skills in order to reduce the amount of mass required in the production of goods and services. The strategies employed by individuals, businesses, and institutions in the shift from mass to information are threefold: they innovate, adapt, or react. The most innovative aspect of this change is the world of microelectronics and the information age it has ushered in.

Industrial technology that began with machines that accomplish or assist manual tasks is extended by the information age to intelligent machines that imitate and assist the mind. The Industrial Revolution created products that replaced physical activity: trains replaced horses; steam engines replaced sailboats; reapers replaced scythes. The information age produces computers that talk, listen to the human voice, print what is said, read handwriting, and communicate with other machines. These innovations have been brought about by the invention and successful application of semiconductors, microprocessors, fiber optics, lasers, and communication satellites. These technologies, when coupled with advances in computer hardware and miniaturization, will become powerful tools in the shift from the mass to the informative economy.

While computers are becoming the new industrial empire, replacing the manufacturing and durable goods sector of the economy, their value to society, we must remember, is in how they allow us to accomplish work quickly, economically, and efficiently. Although the burgeoning world of microelectronics offers many possibilities in terms of new products, services, and entertainment, their primary economic utility is the ability to shift the ratio of mass to information. One of the ways this is accomplished is by changing the procedure of work.

In 1977 Dr. Marc Porat first quantified the percent of GNP that was solely devoted to information services and goods. His study was done for the U.S. Department of Commerce and was based on calculations for 1967. Dr. Porat estimated that 46 percent of the GNP in 1967 was composed of the information sector of the economy. In the "primary information sector," which produced 25 percent of the GNP, people produced such information-providing goods as computers, communications equipment, printing, television, and related activities including advertising, consulting, and data processing. Dr. Porat also estimated that a "secondary information sector" consisting of another 21 percent of the GNP could be found within noninformation-sector businesses such as manufacturing, medicine, and various service industries, representing the total output of information services and goods for use within these areas. Examples are persons in a factory whose job is training new workers, in-house accountants, and data-processing workers.

Because Dr. Porat's study was meticulously and copiously documented, it serves as a definitive measurement of the information sector of the economy some fifteen years ago. What no one knows now is to what extent since then the manufacturing economy has shifted to an informative economy. Obviously, the informative economy has grown. Studies of new job formation during the 1970s estimate that of the 10 million new jobs created, no more than 10 percent were in manufacturing. The balance was in either the service or the information sector of the economy.

But we must remember that the information age cannot make an end run around the industrial mass economy. To succeed, it must include the industrial economy and make it more informed. In order for the manufacturing sectors of our economy to survive and develop during this shift to the informative economy, they will need to adopt the innovations of the information age rapidly and thoroughly. Computers, the "pencils of the 1980s," will be mandatory for any small or large company trying to create efficiency, control, and good communications systems both internally and with their customers. The Japanese were the first to employ microelectronics on the auto assembly line and in the automobile itself. When combined with their lower labor costs, this means they can produce a car for 25 percent less than a similar one made in Detroit or England.

But besides employing these innovative technologies, there are other equally important ways to shift the ratio of mass to information, and these are reflected in the ways individuals and business *adapt* to the changing relationships among labor, capital, and energy. The following are some examples of business and personal strategies that are adaptive. Although more prosaic than a microchip, they show that the informative economy, far from being a mere technological fix, is a way of perceiving and accomplishing things.

Schlitz and Anheuser-Busch: Until nine years ago, Schlitz not only made Milwaukee famous but also made more money for its stockholders than any other brewer in the country. In 1974 Schlitz produced 24 million barrels of beer per year and had a solid and growing market share of 16 percent. Furthermore, Schlitz had the lowest costs of any major producer. As its volume increased, its margins climbed faster than sales growth. After 1974, Schlitz's fortunes tumbled. At that time, inflation was rising and commodity prices soaring. When price controls imposed by President Nixon were lifted, the full impact was felt by Schlitz in its purchasing costs. To restore margins and regain profit growth, the brewery reformulated its beer, substituting corn sugars for barley malt. Despite the fact that the company essentially cheapened the product, Schlitz raised its prices. Instead of concentrating on making a good product, it concentrated on making a good profit. By 1976 sales had started to slump, and they have continued to decline. Several years after the product reformulation, Schlitz reverted to its old recipe, but by then they had lost the loyalty of many of their customers. Today Schlitz has only 8 percent of the market in beer, is losing money, and was recently sold to Stroh, a smaller brewer.

Anheuser-Busch, in contrast, retained its traditional methods of making beer, which include a longer brewing cycle than that of its competitors and the use of more expensive raw materials. Busch has the highest production costs in the industry and prices its products higher than the competition. The result? Busch has increased sales from a 19 percent market share in 1976 to 34 percent today.

There were other differences between the brewers in terms of marketing, management, and product strategy, but a key difference was quality. Schlitz assumed that its customers would either not notice or not care about the change. Quality is part of the information in a product, especially in something as personal and important to people as their beer. By attempting to achieve the lowest production costs at the expense of quality, Schlitz lost out because of a subtle but critically important ratio of mass to information. Both companies are mass producers—but one gave consumers credit for being able to process information intelligently.

Eastern Airlines and Delta: Eastern Airlines is famed for its rudeness. The source of its attitudes toward customers is attributed to Captain Eddie Rickenbacker, the much-decorated flying ace who ran Eastern for twenty-five years. Captain Rickenbacker didn't care as much about passengers as he did about airplanes, and despite his absence since 1959, apparently it takes a long time for entrenched attitudes to change. But rudeness may not be the only problem. By comparison with Delta, Eastern has always lagged in its fleet efficiency, owning planes that were more costly to run, because Eastern has been slower to change models. Because of this, Eastern has had lower profits and consistently higher operating costs per mile than its competitor Delta. This in turn has required Eastern to carry higher levels of debt, so that at $2.0 billion, Eastern has the highest debt of any U.S. airline.

Delta, in contrast, has always been first in line to purchase more efficient airplanes and will soon have the largest fleet of the new Boeing 757s and 767s, which will lower its unit operating costs by 40 percent. Because of its efficiency, Delta has been more profitable and has been able to finance most of its capital improvements through internal cash flow rather than debt. During the last ten years, Delta was the most profitable airline in the United States, with earnings of $949 million, while Eastern lost $29 million during the same period. In addition, Delta is not unionized, but instead has a program, similar to those found in Japanese companies, of lifetime employment. Delta claims that in return for this willingness to carry its employees during periods of slack economic activity, it has higher productivity, in part because people perceive themselves to be a part of one integrated unit and are willing to switch jobs and positions as workload and demands require. Union work rules forbid this kind of flexibility.

The underlying difference between these two airlines can be viewed as the difference between mass and information. Service is information; companies that provide good service win loyalty and favor. During the energy shocks of 1974 and 1979, Delta had in place fuel-efficient aircraft that enabled the company to have substantially lower operating and fuel expenses than the rest of the industry. Delta supposedly sacrifices short-term earnings by depreciating its aircraft sooner but has produced the highest earnings in the airline industry. By purchasing new aircraft that have a high ratio of information to mass, Delta has become the leading U.S. airline.

A Million-Mile Truck: In Iowa, the Ruan Transport Company has designed and has had manufactured a truck for long, cross-continental hauls that can go a million miles before a major overhaul, doubling the existing standard for eighteen-wheelers. To do this, Ruan worked with suppliers to obtain longer-lasting parts and innovative components. Although Ruan is only a leasing agent and trucker, it accomplished what no company has done before: it designed its own truck and had it assembled *without* a factory. It contracted out all work to existing suppliers and component fabricators. The new truck, called the Ruan Mega, costs 20 percent more than the competitive models but is expected to last 50 percent longer and require less maintenance. Ruan expects to have five hundred trucks in operation in 1983.

Toshiba Refrigerators: Toshiba has produced a refrigerator that uses only 70 percent of the electricity employed by the average, comparably equipped American refrigerator of similar size. Since refrigerators are the fourth largest user of electricity, behind air conditioning, lighting, and industrial electric motors, Toshiba refrigerators installed in American homes would save 3 percent of the nation's power, or enough to close down forty nuclear power plants.

Sail Power: Several small companies now design and manufacture sail-assisted boats for transport and fishing. In 1974, when fuel for the fishing fleet was either unavailable or rationed in Seattle, Skookum Marine Construction began designing and building 53-foot fishing boats based on the design of its yachts. Skookum has now built forty-five of the boats and reports that fishermen using the boats save 50 percent in fuel costs because of the sail assist and the more efficient hull design. It has been estimated that it currently costs $1 in fuel for every pound of fish caught. Builder Bernie Arthur of Skookum Marine says, "People here can prove these boats work. They are taking 53-foot boats, which cost $30,000, from Seattle to Midway Island and back on 500 gallons of fuel and bringing in 30,000 pounds of fish, a trip worth about $30,000. You take a big 190-

foot seine boat that costs $10 million and needs a big crew, they'll come in with 100 tons of albacore worth $200,000, but they are using maybe 50,000 gallons of fuel. They know they are in the wrong spot at the wrong time, but what can they do?"

Health and Diet: In 1981 the amount spent on what is euphemistically referred to as health care climbed to an all-time high of 9.8 percent of the GNP, or $287 billion, a per capita expense of $1,275. Further, throughout the past decade, health costs have climbed faster than the growth of the GNP, both in actual expenditures and in rate-of-cost increase. In ten years, from 1971 to 1981, hospital expenses have quadrupled, physician services have climbed three and a half times, and nursing-home costs have more than quadrupled.

These statistics and the fact that diseases are increasingly being correlated with environmental causes (ten years ago only 10 percent of cancers were thought to be environmentally related; today, authorities feel that figure is closer to 90 percent) are causing consumers to switch dietary habits from mass-produced foodstuffs containing high amounts of fat, sugar, and salt to locally produced fresh foods. The shift in eating habits has given rise to less adulterated food, more local greengrocers, and small shops selling freshly made bread, ice cream, or ready-to-eat items. Here again there has been a shift to informatively made products, without the intermediation of advertising, centralized warehousing, and, in this case, chemical preservation. Food products sold and made in small shops have a higher labor component in their final price and usually involve more skilled and intelligent labor than that required by a cannery, production bakery, or packing house.

These may seem like small, inconsequential changes and acts, but as you look at the landscape of the American city, you will notice that this shift from mass to informativeness marks the newer and more successful restaurants, retail shops, and services sprouting up.

Keeping Cars Longer: Between 1970 and 1980, the average age of cars on the road increased from 5.5 years to 6.5 years and is continuing to rise. While automobile manufacturers blame the recession for declining sales, others believe a shift in attitude is occurring. William Prebe, a vice-president of Dana Corporation, an automotive supplier, says, "People don't look at a car as something to show off anymore. Buying a car is like buying a household appliance. You've got to have one, but you'll buy it only when you need it." In the meantime, the automobile parts and repair businesses are thriving and lengthening the useful life of cars. The Commerce Department reports that cars are being driven about 10 percent less per year at slower speeds than they were a decade ago, further extending the life of the car and reducing wear. In the face of these statistics, the chairman of American Motors, the least successful U.S. auto company, has strongly advocated a renewal of "planned obsolescence."

Minimills For Steel: While the American steel industry is reeling from recessions, falling demand, and foreign competition, domestic mills specializing in recycling scrap steel are flourishing. Minimills started by making simple steel products from recycled steel. There are now at least fifty such mills scattered about the country with 13 percent of the total steel market divided among them. Joel Hirschhorn, of the congressional Office of Technology Assessment, thinks they will capture one-fourth of the market by 1990. Minimills use the newer technologies of electric-arc furnaces and continuous casters. Their energy usage per ton of steel is about 9.9 million Btus, while original manufacturers of steel require 35.2 million Btus.

Another means to shift the ratio of mass to information is to *react* by returning to an earlier way of doing things. Primarily an individual response to the stagnation of the mass economy and the high cost of living, this reaction can mean simplifying one's life: making compost out of kitchen scraps instead of having a garbage disposal; having a garden; sewing at home. It can mean a return to barter: exchanging items at swap meets; a baby-sitter co-op; or trading professional services. It can mean cutting back on consumption: eating lower on the food chain by eliminating excessive quantities of meat; not buying processed foods; bicycling instead of driving.

In all industrialized countries, this reaction to the rising costs of sustaining one's standard of living during a time of rising taxes and prices is driving people into what is called the informal, or underground, economy. The words used to describe it invoke the image of something shadowy, illicit, hidden, and less than legal. In part this image is accurate, since the underground economy usually includes the dealings of drug traffickers, criminals, and smugglers. But even if their contribution is excluded from the estimates of the size of the informal economy, it has grown inexorably over the last decade and threatens to engulf the formalized accounting of the mainstream economy.

When the mass economy was growing, it provided a steadily increasing flow of revenues for government activity. Whether countries spend much of their money on welfare, as does England, or on defense, as does the United States, tax revenues have allowed government programs to grow as fast or faster than the economy itself. Post-OPEC inflation created "bracket creep" in countries with progressive taxes. Middle-class taxpayers ended up in upper-middle-class tax brackets as their paychecks rose while in fact real earnings remained steady or declined. But as growth slowed, two forces began to oppose each other.

The first was the decline in the economy, abetted in part by large government spending and deficits, which have crowded out businesses from the capital markets. This lack of reinvestment has caused U.S. business to lose its competitive vigor, reducing the number of jobs at home, further weakening the economy, and decreasing government revenues. The decline of the mass economy in turn caused more people to seek federal, state, and local assistance during times of unemployment and for medical, food, and housing aid. This drives the cost of government higher at a time when revenues are declining, thereby increasing deficits and causing the government to reach ever more deeply into the national piggy bank to finance its activities. In the 1960s, when the structural underpinnings of the mass economy were sound, budget deficits stimulated economic activity, creating new growth and, as a consequence, an easing of government deficits. Now that the mass economy has permanently peaked, deficits only drive the economy deeper into debt.

The informal economy is the individual's response to the crisis of the mass economy. While the mass economy declines, individuals are turning away from the formalized procedures of economic participation, particularly high taxes, because they perceive them to be punitive and unfair. In other words, they are trying to escape the decline of the economy by creating smaller, local, more controllable economies around them. The informal economy is currently estimated to be between 10 and 22 percent of the total GNP of the United States. In Italy it is said to exceed 30 percent and is called the submerged economy. In Germany it is called the shadow economy. Russians call it their second economy, and it may exceed 20 percent of the nation's GNP. In France the *travail au noir* is so large in the construction trades that 50 percent of the cement that is sold cannot be traced to officially recognized building sites.

People are lowering the cost of goods by dealing directly with one another through barter and cash. Mass in the form of capital is reduced; mass is capital in this sense because in order for people to attain the same purchasing power they have through barter or cash dealings they would have to earn more, which in turn would require both more work and more energy. How does informativeness increase? Clearly, in those activities that are illegal the issues of mass and information are not involved. But besides illicit activity and barter, there is in the United States and European countries an aspect of the informal economy that represents voluntary assistance between friends and neighbors as well as self-help and reliance. There is something tantamount to barn raisings occurring throughout the United States—only the tasks have changed. This type of work has been called the "fourth sector" by two German scholars, Dr. Rolf G. Heinze and Thomas Olk, who have studied the *Schattenwirtschaft*, or shadow economy, of West Germany: "The fourth sector can be differentiated from the formal economy by the nature of the work; it is autonomous, the length and division of tasks are decided by the individual; it requires a high degree of labor input and a high level of skill, requires little capital and raw materials, and offers those involved a high degree of job satisfaction. Those who operate in this sector are partly in the formal economy and partly in the informal; sometimes money is exchanged, sometimes goods or services." The fourth sector is the unregistered, untaxed, and unconventionally paid employment that is arising out of unemployment. After all, unemployed people do not all sit home and watch television. In addition to the some 11 million people who are officially unemployed in the United States, as well as the

1.7 million discouraged workers and 5.5 million part-time workers, there are others who long ago chose not to be employed in conventional ways. As they drop between the cracks of conventional government accounting, they are not even missed. And as they find alternate economic pathways that satisfy their needs for income, support, and meaningful work, they expand the societal network and framework for this type of economic behavior.

The implications of the informal economy are damaging to conventional economic theory. In order for economics to operate as a science, it must be able to measure the economy. Without proper measurement, economic theory becomes wildly abstract. Professor Edgar Feige of the University of Wisconsin estimates the total U.S. informal economy at over $700 billion dollars, larger than the GNP of France. Peter Gutmann of Baruch College estimates it to be just over $500 billion, or the size of England's GNP. Pollster Louis Harris puts the figure at $400 billion. But whatever figure is closest, it is large enough to make conventional economic analysis suspect, if not useless. It means that employment is considerably higher than reported, that Americans have more savings than is officially acknowledged, and that real economic growth, while certainly not occurring in the industrial sector, is occurring somewhere and on some basis in the United States. And it is the existence of this economy that may explain why, in 1982, the year of the highest unemployment and business failure since the Depression, there has been hardly any social unrest or agitation. In short, there are two economies in the United States.

❋ Chapter 8
Disintermediation

T he butcher, the baker, and the candlestick maker have become the food systems analyst, the infection control coordinator, and the utility command and control systems engineer. Work, which used to consist of making an object from beginning to end, has become fragmented. From an agrarian society, where economic production was largely self-sufficient and where people spent most of their time producing necessities for themselves, we have become a people who perform only tiny segments of the overall task of production, and we consume mostly what has been produced by others. The change in transportation from foot to horse to train to car to plane has produced an explosion of complex tasks and services. I can walk from New York to Boston by myself. To fly requires the work of tens of thousands of people. This is intermediation.

Between 1870 and 1973 gross world production climbed from \$30 billion to \$4.8 trillion, a fifty-fold increase, even accounting for inflation. The most rapid growth occurred between 1947 and 1973, when gross world production increased an average 4.7 percent per year. Although this economic growth was interrupted by periods of recession and contraction, the overall rate of growth accelerated consistently until 1973. If we can say, somewhat arbitrarily, that the Industrial Revolution began in the mid-eighteenth century, it was not until some two hundred years later, in 1955, that the world produced one trillion dollars' worth of goods in a single year. Ten years later, in 1965, gross world production had doubled. By 1973 it had nearly quintupled.

The rise of industrial civilization has been accompanied by an increasing diversity of complex intermediary institutions whose function is to interconnect all aspects of the ever-growing, expanding world of material civilization. When we refer to the simple days of the past, we think of a life largely devoid of intermediation—no or few taxes, self-sufficiency, interdependence among neighbors, inventiveness, frugality, make-do-or-go-without common sense and practicality. The complexity of modern life is almost entirely the result of our having to deal with and master hundreds of different institutions and situations. Tax forms are difficult, transportation is costly and requires trained mechanics, jobs require intense specialization and professionalization, getting ahead depends on who you know, creating a livelihood involves the mastery of complex markets and production functions.

This rapid economic expansion necessitated (as was discussed in Chapter 1) "intermediation"—the introduction into the economic system of specialized goods, services, and institutions. Banks act as intermediaries in the world of money—handling deposits, making loans, holding reserves, selling certificates of deposit, borrowing from the Federal Reserve Bank. Food processors process, package, preserve, color, and bring food close to our homes. Government agencies act as intermediaries in order to defend, educate, feed, and govern the nation they represent. Every act involves dozens of intermediary functions.

This exponential rise in complexity can be seen through a simple product: shoes. The cobbler made them once, from hides bought at the tannery and nails purchased from the blacksmith. A modern shoe manufacturer, realizing that athletic shoes are in great demand, buys uppers from Korea and soles from Taiwan. To do so, he must constantly be aware of currency fluctuations, rates of duties, and production schedules, which he monitors through Telex and constant travel to Asia. In the United States, to assemble his Taiwanese soles with his Korean uppers, he must use a special adhesive made to adhere to a polyurethane sole. This adhesive, however, contains a solvent that is under scrutiny by the Environmental Protection Agency and the Occupational Safety and Health Agency as a possible carcinogen. His in-house research chemist tries to find another adhesive he can use, while the EPA issues regulations strictly limiting the amount of solvents that he can release into the environment. Meanwhile, OSHA lowers the permissible levels of solvent in the factory to protect employees' health, so the manufacturer must install expensive and specialized air-filtration and removal systems that require the services of an engineering firm located in another state.

To distinguish his shoe from its competitors, the manufacturer must add a unique marking on the side that his lawyer must copyright. Since his hometown lawyer feels this is beyond his expertise, he asks a college friend who is with a large Washington, D.C., firm to carry out the legalities. To market this patented shoe with the potentially toxic glue, the manufacturer must attend at least thirty different sports and shoe trade shows. He has two large display booths that are constantly being shipped by truck from city to city. He has a specially trained staff that spends a lot of its time in hotels and airplanes to meet and attract customers, and he himself must attend the major shows in order to make his big clients feel important. At these shows, however, his main task is to look at what his competitors are doing, including the company in Korea that makes his uppers, because they are now marketing their own brand of shoes. At one show, he notices that athletic shoes are shifting from active use to passive use, from sports to fashion, and he wonders if he should not introduce a line of shoes with softer, more autumnal colors to extend his reach into this growing market. At a competitor's booth, he spots shoes that look remarkably like his and wonders if his Korean supplier is also supplying this company. He makes a note to contact his lawyer and sue for copyright infringement, the fifth time he has had to engage in a lawsuit this year. When he gets back to his hotel, he is told that there will likely be a longshoremen's strike next week, that two ship containers of shoes will be stuck on the water, and that many customers who cannot get their spring orders within the next two or three weeks have threatened to cancel them.

If you own a shoe store. you unknowingly pass on the cost of the shoe manufacturer's lawsuits with every pair of that company's shoes you sell. Similarly, if you own a hardware store, you add the expense of your biannual trips to hardware product conventions to the price of your waffle irons. If you own a corner store, you pass on to your customers the price of brand-name banana advertising with every bunch of bananas. If you, as a consumer, think athletic shoes, waffle irons, and bananas are expensive, you can be sure that the manufacturers of these products, squeezed during the past decade by high interest rates, soaring inflation, rising costs, and softening markets think they are too cheap. The mass economy has become so large and complex, and the activity of intermediation so pervasive, that both consumer and producer are feeling financially squeezed. When the economy was growing and wages were rising, while prices were either steady or falling, manufacturers did not feel so pressed—intermediary goods and services proliferated and were accepted as a cost component in goods. But since 1973 the economy has slowed, and recently it has begun to contract. This slowing of growth has contributed to inflation, high interest rates, and lowered wages. It has also brought into question the value of increased intermediation. Intermediation is a direct result of the growth of the economy's complexity and scale; thus an economy that no longer expands reduces the need for further intermediary goods and services. In many cases—for example, food and clothing—intermediation has become the largest component in the final price paid for goods. While industrial society will always require intermediary agencies to function smoothly, the magnitude of intermediation added to the cost of our goods now far exceeds, in many consumers' minds, the usefulness gained. This reaction leads to the opposite economic action; disintermediation. When consumers began buying generic (no-label) supermarket products after 1973, they were rejecting the cost of brand-name promotion and advertising added to their toilet paper and canned apricots. Out went one of the "middlemen"—Madison Avenue. In this one small way, advertising agencies became disintermediated, signaling the beginning of a continuing, long-lived trend.

The classic example of disintermediation was the creation and growth of the money-market fund. A banking institution is disintermediated when it has to pay more money in interest to attract deposits than it receives in interest from the loans it has made. Prior to the inflationary period of the late seventies, banks and thrift institutions paid 5 and 5¼ percent to depositors while receiving 7 to 10 percent on their automobile and housing loans. As inflation grew more severe after 1974, money-market funds were created, taking pools of capital and purchasing short-term notes (debts) issued by governments, agencies, corporations, and banks. These notes paid far higher interest rates than banks were paying their depositors. These money-market funds issued "shares" at $1 each and passed along— as "dividends" paid directly to shareholders—the interest payments received on the notes. Shareholders could sell their shares back to the fund by writing a check; they had gained both high interest and liquidity—easy access to their money.

As money-market funds proliferated, banks and thrift institutions began to lose deposits, and in an effort to reclaim them, they created new deposit "certificates" and special accounts that paid higher interest than regular savings accounts.

Although banks could adjust to the higher interest costs they were paying by raising interest rates on the loans they made, thrift and savings and loan institutions were stuck with long-term mortgages that paid lower rates of interest. They were disintermediated. Money-market funds had cut out the middleman. Acting as a broker for notes that were being sold on the open market, they, in effect, allowed small depositors to lend money directly to the government and corporations. The money that earned 5 percent in a bank savings account might have been lent by that bank to General Motors. When one buys shares in a money-market fund, the fund uses that money to buy a promissory note from General Motors and passes all but ¼ to ½ percent of the interest back to the money-market shareholder.

Disintermediation covers a far broader range of economic activities than the outflow of funds from thrift institutions. It reduces the number of intermediary steps in the production and distribution of goods and services. Persons, businesses, and organizations who understand and practice disintermediation will prosper and thrive as the contracting economy squeezes out the intermediary activities. While we once could afford the proliferation of middlemen, marketers, and agents, a contracting economy requires economic directness—individuals and businesses can no longer afford the frills. This change raises the ratio of intelligence or information to mass, because if one buys directly from a producer, jobbers, advertisers, printers, salesmen, and retailers have been eliminated. None added information to a product, but all required labor and energy to support their activities.

Disintermediation is one of the principal means by which individuals can sustain a standard of living in a contracting economy. Disintermediation covers products and activities as various as flea markets, paramedical clinics, conservation, and the direct-mail business. It includes all attempts, both legal and illegal, to circumvent the complicated and cumbersome apparatus of the modern market economy, whether the motive is simple self-gain, the avoidance of a taxable transaction, or the skirting of bureaucratic regulations. It consists of any direct transaction or exchange of goods or services that bypasses a middleman, professional, specialist, or institution that is normally involved in such a transaction. Not only is disintermediation becoming commonplace among individuals, but it is suffusing all of commerce, reflecting a strategic adjustment by companies to shrinking sales and rising costs. When someone buys a top-quality tent from Moss in Camden, Maine, he or she is making a decision to buy the finest tent direct from the makers, thus supporting skill and craft but not middlemen. We seem at heart to be a conservative nation, and there is nothing as conservative as buying a durable object at a reasonable price from the people who produced it. Even IBM, with one of the most elaborate, highly trained, and highly paid sales organizations in the world, has recently begun selling its equipment directly to businesses over an "800" toll-free telephone number at a discount on the retail price.

The more highly intermediary an industry, the more likely it is that it will become a target for disintermediation. Utilities are a good example. Inside a $2 billion concrete shell designed to withstand bombs and earthquakes is a nuclear reactor that boils water to produce steam that turns turbines that generate electricity that is sent over high-tension cables for 100 miles to substations that reduce the voltage and resend it across town to a house where an electric can opener opens a tin of beans. The use of nuclear energy is, to borrow physicist Amory Lovin's oft-quoted analogy, like cutting butter with a chain saw.

There is no more violent meeting between intermediation and disintermediation than in the utility industry, where the interests of conservation clash with the costs of enormously expensive nuclear plants. Although many plants recently have been canceled, many others are too far along in construction to be stopped. For years we have been told that nuclear energy would be plentiful and cheap, and now we find that nuclear energy will cost the consumer more than conventionally generated electricity. The Shoreham nuclear power plant in Brookhaven, New York, is expected to increase utility rates for its customers by 30 percent if and when it goes on line in 1983–84. The Grand Gulf nuclear station will raise rates similarly for customers of Mississippi Power & Light. The Wolf Creek nuclear plant will raise Kansas Gas & Electric rates by at least 60 percent when it opens in 1984. These new plants were hit not only by rising construction costs but, more important, by falling demand for electricity.

Increases in utility rates encourage people to use less electricity. In this way, conservation is one of the simplest and most highly disintermediary acts, since it eliminates expansion by utilities while saving energy, capital, and income.

The highly intermediary food business is gradually being disintermediated as more people grow their own. When energy was cheap and the economy was expanding, it was much more economical to buy food than to grow it oneself. However, because increased food production in the United States was accomplished by corresponding increases in energy consumption in the form of fuel, pesticides, fertilizers, and transportation costs, the increase in oil prices has caused corresponding increases in the cost incurred during every stage of food production. In 1982 it cost $2,000–$5,000 to ship a truckload of lettuce from California to the East Coast. In 1910 the amount of energy required to grow 1 calorie of food was estimated to be 1 Btu. Today that figure has risen to at least 10 Btu per calorie of food produced. And since the cost of energy has increased over 5 times in constant dollars since 1910, we have increased the energy cost of each calorie of food by 50 times (10 times increase in amount of energy × 5 times increase in energy cost). In 1981, according to a Gallup poll, 45 million families had gardens in which they grew food worth over $14 billion at retail prices, or approximately 5 percent of the country's total food purchases.

Rising affluence and intermediation—the result of the mass economy—decreased the amount of communication and information exchanged between consumers and producers. Like a secret told around a huge table, the information that went from producer to consumer and back again was thoroughly distorted by the lengthy indirect communication created by our intermediary economy. Communication lines became long as the scale of business increased, and producers had to turn to magazines, radio, and television to communicate with the public. Manufacturers had to shout. But though the media was an effective means for producers to speak to consumers, it became difficult for consumers to talk back. Companies heard only their own voices and spent much of their revenues creating and maintaining consumer demand. This is still true today, but the situation is changing. Consumers have become suspicious and cynical. They now see size— once an assurance of quality—as a likely sign of indifference. When economic expansion was increasing rapidly, the problems of big business had less to do with consumer attitudes than with capitalization, advertising, and efficient management. The launching of a new product by Procter & Gamble, regarded as the premier consumer marketing company in the world, is an example of how crucial it has become for companies to get back in touch with their customers.

For the past eight years, Procter & Gamble has tried valiantly to get Americans to eat Pringles, a highly processed potato chip pressed flat in a can. Although potato chips rate low on any nutritional scorecard, their components are (or were) minimal: potatoes, oil, and salt. Pringles, packaged with a Gay Nineties logo, require a paragraph to list their various ingredients and additives. Procter & Gamble, according to the senior vice-president of the Wall Street brokerage firm Drexel Burnham Lambert, has spent $300 million in the unsuccessful development of Pringles and has lost more than $200 million. Since the introduction of Pringles in 1975, the marketplace has been clearly indicating it wants food products that are less manipulated and contrived. Procter & Gamble, as intelligent as they are in their management practices, has refused to heed their customers, and thus Pringles remains a classic corporate exercise in waste and excess.

Although in the past consumers have not had the direct access to large corporations that the corporations have had to consumers, the situation is changing because of disintermediation. In retailing, the disintermediary business is mail-order. Today, there are

8,000 companies doing $40 billion in sales. Customers are discovering that they can obtain high-quality products at reasonable prices with good service through the mails. Retail establishments were once highly service-oriented, but now patrons of large department stores and retail outlets complain about the lack of help, service, and information. A reporter for the *Wall Street Journal* noticed that in one of the vast emporiums of a national chain he could not find one sales-person in all 50,000 square feet of store space. When queried, the manager said he saw no reason to have salespeople when his customers knew more than his help. Small, specialized mail-order companies fill this void by creating catalogues and businesses that are highly informative, with staff and personnel who know their product lines well. Most of these companies accept returns without question. L. L. Bean accepted a thirty-three-year-old sweater from a customer who thought it had developed a flaw and promptly sent him a new one.

Disintermediation is having an impact on the professions. Vocationally, intermediation is synonymous with overspecialization. The rapid expansion of the economy required us to restrict our focus to narrow niches and become consumers of each other's specialties. Disintermediary livelihoods can be described as activities that cut across the narrowness and specialization of law, medicine, and education. Midwives have proliferated during the past twelve years to more than 10,000, disintermediating the power that obstetricians and gynecologists have had over women and birth. Midwives are generally more sensitive to women than physicians, spend more time before and after the birth with their clients, and work with husbands to make the birth a family experience. For healthy mothers, midwives, performing home deliveries and charging $300 to $500, are cheaper than the $1,500 to $2,000 hospital birth costs.

The growth of the paralegal profession helps people deal with the law without the costly and often time-consuming intermediation of a professional lawyer. Nolo Press, a company created by two lawyers, has put out a series of books that show people, among other things, how to file their own divorces, form their own corporations, avoid probates, patent computer software, file for bankruptcy, and go to small-claims court. Written and edited by trained lawyers, these books are disintermediating the overprofessionalism and legislative complexity that has kept most people from reasonably priced access to the legal process. Their most recent title is *29 Reasons Not to Go to Law School*. The books have been remarkably successful, and they are a demonstration of another disintermediary phenomenon: the rise of the small press.

Not only individuals but also corporations are seeking means to avoid the erosive and expensive process of litigation. Last year, Fortune 500 companies spent $2.5 billion in legal fees. The adversary system of adjudication that prevails in commercial law promotes lengthy trials, appeals, and obfuscation because lawyers are paid for the time required rather than the results produced. To avoid this, corporations such as TRW and Aetna are using alternative means to settle disputes, including minitrials, the hiring of private judges, and arbitration and mediation. A company called Endispute, Inc., based in Washington, D.C., has been formed to help companies find other methods of conflict resolution. The American Arbitration Association reports that its disputes require only one-fourth the amount of time to settle compared with the time needed by civil courts. Furthermore, mediation experts estimate that legal costs constitute only one-tenth the costs of court battles.

In education and medicine, an example of disintermediation exists in the magazine edited by Dr. Thomas Ferguson. Entitled *Medical Self-Care*, the quarterly magazine assists people in gaining greater control over their lives, health, and doctor bills. Written by experienced health professionals, the magazine helps readers save money, teaches them basic medical skills, stresses the preventive advantages of exercise and nutrition, and advises how and when to use a doctor. This amounts to another example of a do-it-yourself movement that unites previously separate aspects of our lives. *Medical Self-Care* estimates that 80 percent of our existing medical expenses are avoidable. By making its readers medically more knowledgeable with each issue, it is eliminating for them much of the vast, industrialized medical systems that have subsumed the healing arts.

Without doubt, disintermediation is most easily accomplished in small businesses and organizations. Because there is a widespread belief that small businesses are not what is going to save our country from economic decline, little attention is paid to them, while inordinate attention is paid to large corporations. Nevertheless, despite all the mergers, buy-outs, and corporate acquisitions of the past ten years, the five hundred largest industrial corporations employ 15.6 million people—no more than they did ten years ago. Jobs are critical to the well-being of the nation, and the creation of jobs is vital to economic security. During the past ten years, two-thirds of all new jobs were created in businesses with less than twenty employees. Over 80 percent of the jobs for young blacks, the group with a 49 percent unemployment rate, are provided by small companies. A recent National Science Foundation study determined that small companies produce twenty-four times as many industrial innovations per research dollar as do large companies.

Disintermediation can also mean a change in which the production of goods or rendering of service is more closely integrated with consumption. An example of this sort of disintermediation was the 1982 proposal by the city of San Jose, California, to institute its own fire-insurance program—a simple idea with far-reaching ramifications.

The city researched what homeowners and businesses were spending annually on fire insurance. Looking at its own actuarial statistics, the city determined it could provide the same insurance and save $25 million yearly for policyholders. In addition, the income from selling the fire insurance would pay for the city's entire fire department. For both citizens and their government, it was an obvious win-win situation: citizens would pay less for insurance, governments would receive more money, and taxes could, theoretically, be lowered. But there are more benefits to this idea than just the obvious economic one. By providing its own fire insurance, the city, through its fire department, would have the incentive to promote safety programs, increased fire inspections, and the elimination of fire hazards. Citizens, once they began to understand that fewer fires would mean lower premiums, would have an additional incentive to increase their own concern about fire and safety.

If San Jose creates its own insurance company, it will create approximately as many jobs as will be lost by the changeover in the insurance capitals of Omaha and Hartford. But, what is more important is that the meaning of those jobs will change. Local sales agents of an insurance company feel and express concern about their community, while a person working in a large office complex in Hartford is hard put to feel directly involved with a city 3,000 miles away. Another benefit is that money will go back into the community. San Jose could publish a statement of its income and expenditures from its fire-insurance venture, and, instead of loaning the insurance-premium money it takes in to a Texas developer building a high rise in Dallas (as a "national" insurance company might do), the city could see that the money is put back into San Jose.

Companies can disintermediate themselves. While IBM is doing so by selling directly through an "800" number, smaller technology companies are also catching on. Tektronix, Inc., based in Oregon, is one of the leading manufacturers of oscilloscopes. In recent years, it has been hit with aggressive Japanese competition, which has kept prices lower. For one of its oscilloscopes, a $1,200 model, the company found that it could not afford the expense of separate sales calls, regardless of whether every visit produced a sale or not. So the Australian branch is marketing them directly in technical journals. Customers can send in an enclosed postcard to receive more information and then order directly. The Australian branch sold $100,000 worth of oscilloscopes in six months, and the program is now being implemented in the United States.

General Electric has introduced a repair system for its five major household appliances that appliance owners can follow themselves instead of having to call repairmen. The company has issued repair manuals for each appliance type—refrigerators, ranges/ovens, dishwashers, washers, and dryers. Each manual provides diagnostic information and refers the owners to individual repair systems that are available at appliance stores. The repair system contains all the necessary parts and directions and tells how many minutes and what tools will be required to do the job. If owners get stuck, there is a free "800" phone number they can call seven days a week for assistance.

Arco stations, like all other gas stations, used to accept credit cards, including their own. As handy as credit cards are, they are an enormous intermediary institution, raising the costs of products by 2 to 4 percent. Last March, Arco announced that it was going back to an all-cash system and was lowering prices. Sales increased 50 percent. Where the average service station in the United States sells 42,000 gallons per month, Arco stations average 106,000 per month. Six months after it had instituted the system, Arco was the only major oil company in the United States to show a significant profit increase.

Sometimes disintermediation is brought about by the force of circumstances. In 1982, tuna fishermen in Sausalito, California, found that the San Diego canneries to which they normally sold their catch had already purchased large amounts of Japanese albacore and couldn't take the local catch. So fishermen and their families set up "tuna stands" throughout the San Francisco Bay area and sold the tuna directly to consumers for $1 per pound. Makeshift signs appeared, wives went on the radio and printed up recipes, fishermen gave tips on freezing, thawing, and barbecuing, and some even gave cooking lessons right on the dock. The other side of the story is that the fishermen approached local institutions such as prisons and public agencies to see if they were interested. They weren't, because they had already purchased imported canned tuna at two times the price.

Another example of disintermediation in California that has spread across the country is Owner-Builder Centers. In 1981, 148,000 houses were built by owners, 24,000 more than were built for owners who hired contractors. Owner-Builder Centers teach how to construct, remodel, or add on to a home. As housing prices have soared beyond the reach of many people, thousands are building their own to save money. The centers estimate that an owner can save at least 20 percent by doing the contracting. If the owner is willing to do some or all of the work, the savings can amount to between 44 and 58 percent.

Another kind of intermediation is the formation of special interest groups, professional societies, and trade organizations that have been organized to promote their own interests. Mancur Olson, in his book *The Rise and Decline of Nations*, describes the proliferation of these

types of self-interest groups as a kind of sclerotic clog-
ging of the economic arteries. Their narrow interests
do not always parallel the needs of society as a whole,
and thus their collective effect is to cause the larger
economy to function with many small collusions, laws,
and codes that only benefit a minority at the expense
of the many. Economic expansion has created thousands of intermediary niches, professions, and businesses. They can be expected to fight any social or
economic change that would lessen their influence and
to particularly oppose any disintermediary act or function that undercut their authority. Thus, midwifery has
been decried by the AMA and by obstetricians; energy
conservation was at first ridiculed by the utility companies. During the past three years, the utilities, having
discovered that it is cheaper to encourage conservation
than to build new power plants, have reversed their
opposition. Oil company lobbyists fiercely defend their
own tax breaks, such as oil depreciation allowances,
while criticizing those that would benefit renewable
energy sources, such as wind and solar power, as being
too expensive.

Nevertheless, disintermediation is increasing dramatically in every sector of the economy. Under the
Securities and Exchange Commission's new shelf-reg-
istration ruling, companies can take securities directly
to the market and bypass underwriting firms by selling
directly to investors. Hospitals are teaching "home
care" classes and recommending that patients leave
immediately even after major surgery, to avoid expense and promote faster healing. Biotechnologies will
change the nature of manufacturing in the chemical
industries, eliminating costly raw materials and processes. Electronic banking is blanketing the country
with automatic tellers, eliminating the need for branch
offices; self-service gas pumps are being installed; and
banking at home through personal computers is being
offered by Crocker Bank.

The signs of the transition from a more intermediary to a more disintermediary economy are all around us, but are perceived variously by different people. It is easy to dismiss the informative economy because it is difficult to pin down. It has no business page, hardly any magazines, and no indices of its own. It is difficult to measure in economic terms a home birth or the durability of a product.

Against the ebbing of mass economic activity, the present administration has attempted to implement a broad economic program. Washington assumes that there is a "normal" economy to return to and that we can restore overall growth, prosperity, and productivity without the pain of inflation or contraction. The administration blames the country's stagnation and economic woes primarily on the government itself: the high cost of regulation, swollen bureaucracies, confiscatory taxes, and past deficits. But the argument seems specious, for we are asked to believe that our government, and virtually every other government in the Western world, has blundered, and that each, irrespective of its form, has thrown sand into the gears of its own economy. The mass economy created problems that had not been predicted by any previous economy or social configuration. Before large-scale production of toxic substances, no one proposed an Environmental Protection Agency. To blame the high cost of chemicals and the sad state of the chemical industry on the EPA is to turn cause and effect upside down. Growth of government was a result of growth of industry. That the government engages in waste, gross ineptitude, and bureaucratic foot-shuffling is undeniable, but the government, with its many tax laws and business regulations, is not the cause of slow economic growth, no matter what politicians may say. Nor could the elimination of government solve our economic problems.

Any new governmental policy or economic theory

that tries to reproduce the rapid economic growth of the past will fail. A world that has relentlessly expanded its production of goods and materials for one hundred years has run into limits, and fiscal tinkering is neither the cause of those limits nor their cure. The mass economists are saying that we don't have to change, but the real world is saying that we do. The informative view says that we have to change because the world is on an unalterable course for many decades ahead: an ever-increasing population and slowly declining resources.

This is why the world appears to be giving us contradictory messages. It seems to be going in two directions at once—and it is: toward concentration of resources, capital, and power as the mass economy tries to re-create its historical growth patterns, and toward disintermediation and adaptation. Both are adjustments to similar phenomena—the first to corporations' poor rate of return on their investments in existing plants, machinery, and assets; the second to the poor rate of return individuals are receiving from their work. Therefore, individuals and corporations are changing their strategies. Corporations have been buying undervalued companies, thereby concentrating economic power. Individuals are bypassing, wherever possible, such economic concentration by disintermediating those institutions. In the end, I think it is the individual who will gain the upper hand because it is people, not corporations, that create economies.

❋ Chapter 9

Seven Ways to Think About Your Money

Most of us find ourselves confronted with the need to make decisions about what to do with our money. Even small amounts require careful attention, and in the past ten years the simple task of saving money has become complex and demanding. Some people, either through inheritance or work, do have large amounts of money and must make decisions as to where to place and invest these sums. This chapter is intended to help you look at your money and investments from the point of view of the shift from a mass economy to an informative economy. All of these thoughts are offered with one consideration in mind: during the next decade, the trick will be not to *make* money but to *keep* what you already have. If you do that, you may do better than most.

Borrowers will subsidize savers.

At the beginning of a decade, the financial markets often signal the overall trend of the coming ten years. Why this is true, I do not know. But just as seasons do not suddenly change, markets do not veer in a new direction without giving identifiable signs. Despite the volatility of stock and financial markets, when examined over time, they seem transparent and obvious. There were signs aplenty before the stock-market crash of 1929, but they were largely ignored or, to use a more popular phrase, discounted. In 1928, during a period of rapid real-estate inflation, George Hartford of A&P, against conventional wisdom, decided he would not sign any long-term leases, which supposedly would save him money as rents on real estate escalated. Instead, he changed all the leases of his approximately three thousand stores to a period of one year, reasoning that prices would have to fall. People thought he was mad. A little more than a year later, Hartford renegotiated all his leases, sometimes for as little as 10 cents on the dollar, when real-estate prices crashed along with the stock market.

In 1928 and 1929 Roger Babson, a theologian, economist, and educator, predicted that the Dow Jones would plummet and that "factories will shut down...men will be thrown out of work...the vicious circle will go into full swing and the result will be a serious business depression." Babson was dubbed the "Sage of Wellesley" and denounced by Barron's.

But signals are not all bad. In 1950 and 1960 the market said to buy stocks, and those who did realized handsome gains, if they sold them before 1969. Stock values quadrupled in nineteen years. At the beginning of the seventies, some analysts and writers said to get out of stocks, bonds, and American dollars and buy hard assets or currencies such as gold, real estate, and Swiss francs. The idea of buying gold or silver sounded primitive, even ludicrous, to middle-class sensibilities. Those giving the advice were jeered at in the financial world. But hard assets, including precious metals, farmland, diamonds, and paintings, did very well as long as they were sold before the end of 1979. With the appointment of Paul Volcker to the Federal Reserve in mid-1979, an entirely new direction was signaled, and an economic trend as old as this century abruptly ceased.

For most of the past eight decades, savers have subsidized borrowers. People who put their money in banks and savings and loan institutions earned less money than those who invested in real estate, equities, and industry. (The exception, of course, was the Depression, when losses were widespread.) This was especially true of the period from 1950 to the end of the 1970s, as first growth in equities and later in real estate far outstripped the after-tax return on capital placed in interest-bearing accounts. During this time "smart money" was leveraged by borrowing and parlaying someone else's cash into appreciating assets. The difference between what borrowers and savers were earning was acceptable, as those who saved took little risk while those who borrowed ran the risk of losing their money. As inflation increased during the 1970s, the spread grew broader between what savers were being paid and the rate at which inflating assets, such as real estate, were appreciating. Borrowing money in the late seventies was like minting money until, by 1980, savers began to realize that getting a 5¼ percent return on a savings account was the safest way to *lose* money. Since then, savers subsidizing borrowers has changed to borrowers subsidizing savers. Interest rates have climbed and, since 1980, have been significantly higher than the rate of inflation. So while the markets said to buy stocks in the 1960s and assets in the 1970s, they have been telling us for three years to have cash in the eighties. Be liquid, keep debt low, lend, but don't borrow too much. As I write, we are well into the decade, but the signals are still not understood.

The fact that savers are no longer subsidizing borrowers reveals more about the economy than most people would probably care to know. But if you are going to invest in the coming decade, you must understand why this is occurring.

As discussed in Chapter 4, there have been long periods in the United States marked by growth and expansion and resulting, toward the end of the cycles, in inflation. These have been followed by periods of consolidation, liquidation, and deflation. As growth stopped, demand fell, prices plummeted, and the large debts that had been built up by corporations, foreign countries, mortgagees, and others became unsupportable. When this occurs, bankruptcies, liquidations, and insolvencies feed on each other and produce a long period of economic contraction which sets the stage for the next period of growth and change.

We have unquestionably experienced a long period of growth and expansion, stretching from World War II until 1973. Between 1973 and 1980 there was a period of inflation. The question to ask now is whether we are about to begin a long period of deflation, as has happened before when debt soared and economic growth stopped. No one knows for sure. But the fact that a long trend of savers subsidizing borrowers has reversed is an ominous signal. It means that the demand for cash is increasing. Coming, however, during a time of no economic growth, this means that money is being borrowed so that businesses and individuals can stay alive, not grow.

When the forces of growth are strong, money is loaned at reasonable rates and can be easily repaid out of the profits and earnings generated by growth. When the force of contraction is strong, money cannot easily be repaid, because there is little growth or expansion. Businesses must borrow to survive, which places increased pressure on interest rates. This is happening today, and thus the reversal in the trend of subsidization is an accurate signal that the economy has reached a critical turning point in its development—expansion has changed to contraction.

In the fall of 1982 a heralded drop in interest rates occurred. Short-term rates dropped from 15 to 8 percent, and long-term rates also fell, from 16 percent to 12 percent. Does this undermine what I have said? No, because the critical rate to watch is the *difference* between the rate of inflation and the rate of long-term corporate bonds. This difference is called the "real" interest rate and for most of this century, it has hardly exceeded 2 to 3 percent. In January 1983, despite the drop in nominal interest rates, the real rate was the difference between the 4 percent inflation rate and the 12 percent corporate long-term rate.

Recommendations: This change in the relationship between borrowers and savers signals a long period during which corporations will be liquidating their assets—in effect, getting smaller. If you invest in stocks, don't choose a company that is pretending to get larger when in fact it is contracting. In February 1981 *Forbes* magazine published an article titled "Are More Chryslers in the Offing?" In it, author Richard Greene looked at the analytical methods employed by Kidder, Peabody to determine the cash flow of companies rather than their stated earnings. Cash flow is cookie-jar accounting: it is the total cash income minus total cash expenditures. It tells you at the end of an accounting period whether you have more or less cash than when you started. In addition to computing the companies' actual cash flow, to take into account inflation and replacement costs, Kidder, Peabody also included the amount of money the companies *should* be allowing for depreciation of their plants and equipment. What they came up with was startling.

After analyzing twenty of the thirty companies that make up Dow Jones, Kidder, Peabody found that eleven had negative distributable cash flows. In other words, technically these companies couldn't pay dividends. For example, between 1975 and 1979, U.S. Steel had a negative cash flow of $6.6 billion, and yet they paid dividends. Where did they get the money? By borrowing. But they weren't alone. They were joined by Alcoa, Bethlehem Steel, General Motors, Goodyear, International Harvester, Manville, and Sears. Companies are borrowing to maintain dividend payments in order to keep up the price of their stock, while internally they are actually contracting.

Debt will continue to grow faster than supposed economic growth, and with it will grow interest rates. The wisest action individuals and business can take is to reduce their debt as much as possible. Does this include mortgages? Absolutely. Don't be fooled by the fact that interest on mortgages can be deducted from taxes, effectively lowering interest rates. Debt is debt, and unlike income, assets, and property, it does not depreciate or fall. It is stubborn stuff, and grows with every passing day.

There are two economic forces in violent opposition: deflation and inflation.

The natural tendency of an economy plagued by too much debt and too little growth is to deflate, because as demand falls, so too do the prices of commodities and manufactured products. In the United States, the amounts of consumer, corporate, farm, and government debt have become staggering and are growing rapidly. Third World debt to U.S. banks is growing even faster. Meanwhile, the world economy has stagnated for three years, placing pressure on prices as producers compete for a shrinking market.

The way to avoid deflation is to inflate the currency—to put new money into the system, which dilutes the amount of debt actually owed. Because both deflation and inflation are politically and economically unacceptable, we are seeing national governments seesaw from one monetary policy to another, hoping to find a point that will avoid both. But this is not possible. To grow, the economy requires cash. But even given the stimulative deficits of the past eight years, the U.S. economy has grown anemically by conventional standards. The period during which it reportedly grew, 1976–79, required so much monetary stimulation that high inflation resulted. Monetary restraint practiced since 1979 has resulted in high unemployment, record business failures, and a severely weakened economy. The situation is the same in Europe and is starting to occur in Japan.

Each successive swing in policy produces weaker growth but a stronger inflationary movement. In other words, the economy is becoming more volatile, and this occurs when the forces of deflation and inflation meet like cold and hot air.

Recommendations: Until you can tell with assurance what national and international economic policy will be, most investments will be risky. If you bet on inflation and are wrong, you will lose. If you think the world will deflate, and then rapid inflation takes hold, you will also lose. The most prudent action is to stand in a neutral corner and wait. This will be hard to do, because the turbulence will produce rapid movement in markets. During this period the value of stocks, commodities, and bonds will rise and fall like a rollercoaster. Every time one of the markets soars, as gold did in 1979 and stocks in the fall of 1982, the temptation is to get aboard. But be patient.

I do not recommend any investment at all until you have saved one years' income. Without this cushion to fall back on, such investments as stocks, bonds, and real estate do not make sense because they will put your capital at risk. Your savings should be in the most conservative form possible, and that is U.S. Treasury securities. I recommend a rough 70:30 mix of Treasury bills and notes. Treasury bills are short-term borrowings by the U.S. government and have maturities of 13, 26, and 52 weeks. Treasury bills usually pay one to two percent less than money-market funds and are sold in $10,000 denominations. Treasury notes are generally two- to ten-year obligations, and they generally pay slightly higher rates of interest. They are sold in denominations of $5,000.

The virtue of Treasury securities is the utter absence of risk. At this point in our economy, it makes sense to save money in this form, since the purpose of savings is to preserve capital. If you cannot afford these denominations, then the best way to secure your savings is to place them in a money-market fund that buys only Treasury bills and notes.

Don't invest in fear and greed.

In recent years many books have been published about the economy, quite a number of them best-sellers written from a "survivalist" point of view. These books talk about hyperinflation, currency collapses, and the coming depression, which will sweep all before it in a paralyzing crash of unprecedented proportions. These books often contain prescient and discerning critiques of governmental fiscal and monetary policy and loudly proclaim the lack of clothing on the emperor. At the same time, the authors usually base their investment strategy on two emotions that are incompatible with your investments: fear and greed.

The foremost goal of investing is to preserve your assets—to put the money someplace where, at a later date, you can expect to find that it has kept its value. The second important consideration is to keep it in a form that you can spend or easily change into spendable currency. Next comes the consideration of appreciation, the desire to see money invested in something that will grow and develop.

Fear leads to greed. If you are afraid that your money will be lost because of government bungling, then so-called reactive investments make sense. These include gold, silver, penny stocks, tangibles such as diamonds, and strategic metals. In any market, there is money to be made and lost. Prices go up and down, and some people make fortunes. But reactive investing is closer to speculating, and speculating is a demanding profession not to be undertaken casually.

The most important single question an investor can ask is what the purpose of his or her life is, not what the purpose of money is. Too many people start with the second question and arrive at the conclusion that the role of money is to increase. Investments should first be assessed for what they *do to the investor*. Does an investment make you feel more secure? Does it support an entity or activity that you wish to see benefit by the investment? Investing means placing capital in order to gain profit or advantage; it also means, according to the *American Heritage Dictionary*, to "provide some pervasive quality." Does a particular investment provide the investor with a sense that his or her life is developing, expanding? These are not questions stockbrokers or survivalists will ask. It is all the more important, therefore, to ask them of yourself.

Recommendation: Do not invest unless you personally understand the investment, have some experience with it, and can undertake the investment without worrying.

Buy intelligence before stocks.

If you have unbounded faith in your stockbroker, good. But remember that most brokers do not risk their own capital in the investments they recommend. They are salespeople who benefit not from capital appreciation but from fees earned in the buying and selling of securities. Good brokers not only are few and far between but are generally inaccessible to the small investor because they do better handling large portfolios. It has been shown that throwing darts at the financial pages is as good a way to select stocks as calling on a stockbroker. I am not suggesting a random walk through Standard & Poor's, but I do recommend a sober appraisal of your ability to do well in an area where your expertise is minimal compared with that of professionals. This is true in virtually every investment area, and it is a chastening realization. People often place their money in the hands of others, thinking the broker knows something they don't and hoping their capital will appreciate as if by magic. In so doing they often forget that the best place to put their capital may be in what they know, what they do, and how they live. Scott Burns, author of *Home, Inc.*, has pointed out that since 1974 storm windows installed in a home in the northern United States have consistently provided a better rate of return than AAA-rated bonds and the Dow Jones stocks.

Undoubtedly there has been more written about the stock market than about virtually any other form of investment in the world. The trading of shares is a multibillion-dollar industry, and despite the weak performance of the stock market during the 1970s, it has not lost its seductiveness for many investors. The peak in stock prices occurred in 1966. By the beginning of 1982 the New York Stock Exchange composite index had declined 55 percent, when adjusted for inflation. During this time the rate of return earned through dividends on the stocks that constitute the Dow Jones averages was less than one-half the return of AAA-rated bonds, but this has not deterred touts and analysts from predicting that the bull market of the century is about to begin.

The United States is now in its third serious recession in eight years, one that has seen a decline in the value of stocks, real estate, commodities, and other tangible assets. Inflation is slowing down—a result of the Federal Reserve Board's policy of restricted monetary growth since 1979. But that unwavering policy changed in August 1982, when the financial world was rocked by a series of disturbing events: bank failures, including Penn Square in the United States and Banco Ambrosiano in Italy; the collapse of Drysdale Securities and Lombard-Wall on Wall Street; and the near bankruptcy of Mexico, the largest single creditor to U.S. banks among Third World countries. These events signaled to both the Federal Reserve Board and the markets that the world financial structure was edging toward possible collapse, and that such fragility warranted immediate relief. This relief was supplied by the Federal Reserve in the form of large injections of money into the financial system, along with several cuts in the federal discount rate, the rate at which banks borrow money from the Federal Reserve. In the process, the Federal Reserve underlined the dilemma that faces the United States and the world: If a tight monetary policy is pursued by governments, the lack of fresh stimulus could drive the economy to collapse because of the enormous buildup of debt, accrued by virtually every part of the economy, at a level that could not be paid by a contracting economy. That debt would destroy the financial system as we know it. If, instead, the Federal Reserve begins to pump financial reserves into the system and repeats the chain of events that caused the double-digit inflation of the seventies, inflation could renew itself with a severity that would make past inflationary periods seem tepid. If inflation does begin to heat up again, most people will find it difficult to believe that there will ever be a "normal" economy in the forseeable future, and this would be a psychological catastrophe for the nation.

In the early seventies, many people who analyzed the fiscal policies of Presidents Johnson and Nixon correctly predicted inflation and advised their customers to put their money into such investment hedges as Swiss francs and gold. This time, with many of these former investments having already experienced their "once in a lifetime" surge, the attention would be on stocks.

In the fall of 1982 stocks experienced a historically quick run-up from 776 to 1,065 on the Dow Jones. This may have been, in fact, the beginning of "the" bull market, one that could take the Dow Jones far beyond its recent highs. Whether or not the August to November 1982 rally was the beginning, a powerful, sweeping bull market in stocks will signal a most dangerous time in the economy. Only bull markets, having achieved extraordinary gains in a short time, are susceptible to collapse.

Anyone who bought something during the mid-seventies—a good car, some land, a house—came out looking like a hero, while anyone who scrimped and saved and faithfully put his money into a savings account looked like a fool. In a bull market, many people would try to look like heroes, and there would be steep run-ups in share prices. The Dow Jones average could rise to 2,000; people would feel flush with growing assets.

In such an environment it would be extremely difficult to resist investing in the stock market, because it would provide a demonstrable way to make money in a world where making money has become difficult. If you feel you must invest, do so with great care. The coming bull market is not an ordinary bull market, and it warrants caution. If there is a run-up, it will not herald the recovery promised and hoped for by so many economists and analysts. It is far more likely to be the sunset effect of the mass economic cycle rather than a serious rise in values generated by improvements in economic health and performance. If and when there is such a prolonged rise in the equity markets, I would expect it to last no more than twelve to sixteen months, though it could endure for from twenty-four to thirty months. The length of the rise will be dictated by the rapidity of its rise. The more rapid and sharp the rise, the shorter it will be. Be vigilant, and interpret such volatile happenings warily. Avoid being caught up in the speculative fervor that always accompanies such run-ups. Well before the market passes its zenith, you will want to step aside—not an easy thing to do.

Recommendations: If you invest in the stock market, invest in intelligence first. Instead of investing in individual stocks, I would invest in the market by purchasing shares in mutual funds. *Forbes* magazine publishes every year a recapitulation of the performance of all the major funds with their investment records going back five and ten years, in both down and up markets. A fund I can recommend is the Fidelity Group, particularly its Equity/Income and Magellan funds. Fidelity (82 Devonshire, Boston, Massachusetts 02103) is run by an old Yankee family that knows how to stick to business. But there are many others that are equally well managed.

> *Gold is a store of value,*
> *not an investment.*

Sometimes I think everyone should buy and sell some gold just to get it out of his system—and after that ignore it. Unfortunately, because gold is one of the oldest forms of money, its appeal is not likely to lessen. It is easier to put our trust in the solidity of gold than in the solidity of governments' economic policies. To know why we have become so fascinated with gold, you might take out a dollar bill and read it. It says "Federal Reserve Note." That means it is a note from the Federal Reserve, which guarantees that the piece of paper is worth a dollar. Because most of us are too young to have experienced or witnessed a financial panic, we think little about this statement. But deep in our culture there remains a profound distrust, passed down to us from our elders, of "funny" money that has no backing, meaning, or substance other than as a "note." That mistrust is not unreasonable, because throughout history, governments time and again have created too much inflated money and holders of such "notes" have become impoverished overnight through no fault of their own. In August 1982 the wire services ran a picture of a Mexican woman weeping inside a Tijuana bank after she learned that the money she had saved since 1966 picking tomatoes had lost 75 percent of its value when the Mexican government devalued the peso.

It is not surprising that as inflation heated up in the seventies, many people bought gold. If you feel strongly about having a store of value, you should buy gold and hold it. What gives our currency value is an increasingly tenuous and fragile agreement that even bankers refer to as a giant confidence game. As long as the agreement lasts, currency is valuable. But if the economy should falter badly or be hit by a series of national and international defaults, the likelihood is that the lender of last resort, the federal government, will step in and provide new funds to prevent the system from collapsing. These funds might prove to be highly inflationary, in which case gold would prove to be a valuable insurance policy. But if you do buy gold, look upon it as you do insurance policies for fire and

accidents, policies on which you hope you'll never
have to collect. As soon as you start investing in South
African gold shares, speculating in hard metals, or buying call options on mining stocks, you are counting on
things going wrong in order to benefit personally. Gold
goes up in value when there is social strife, fear of or
actual monetary collapse, and war. It goes down when
the world seems peaceful and orderly. By speculating
in gold, you are placing capital, which is both the sym-
bolic and actual representation of one's work, in an
investment that depends on conflict, crisis, or suffering
in order to be profitable. Speculating in gold isolates
and alienates the speculator, because it is an act that
has no benefit for others.

Recommendations: If you have extra cash to save, and
you want to save in some form other than money, gold
is a way to do so. However, remember that your livelihood and skills are far more important sources of future
security than gold. You might do better to take whatever money you want to place in gold and put
it into your own training and education. When the
Weimar Republic collapsed in 1933 after devastating
hyperinflation, professionals and tradespeople hardly
broke their stride and soon were earning handsome
incomes, had houses, and were solvent. Speculators
were ruined.

Bonds are no longer promises.

Bonds are obligations to those who hold them to repay
the face amount of the bonds together with interest
over the term of the bond. During their life, bonds are
bought and sold, and their face value will vary according to prevailing interest rates. When one buys a
bond, one is lending money on a long-term basis. A
bond carries with it a coupon value or interest rate, an

amount that is paid to the bondholder every quarter. At the end of the term on a bond, the bondholder is paid back the full face value of the bond. For example, if in 1970 you purchased an AT&T thirty-year bond for $1,000 that paid an annual rate of 5 percent interest, you would receive $50 a year until the year 2000, when you would receive your $1,000 back. Since 1970, interest rates have climbed, and a new AT&T bond pays 11 percent interest. In order for your $1,000 bond to yield 11 percent, it would either have to pay $110 a year or have a face value of $454 on the New York Exchange Bond Market. And if you look at what bonds are trading for, you will see that few are now worth their original face value. Of course, if you do not sell the bond, no actual loss will be incurred. What you lose instead is the potential income from an investment yielding a higher rate of return.

Bonds used to be the paragon of conservative investing. Little old ladies were counseled to buy corporate and municipal bonds for safety, security, and stability. That is no longer the case. Because of the rising cost of capital, bonds have become volatile and have plummeted in value since 1979. The decision to invest in bonds is a guess as to whether there will be inflation or deflation. If there is deflation, bonds are a great investment because their face value will appreciate as interest rates fall, and yet they will still be paying high interest rates on the investment. If there is inflation, they will fall further in value and their present rate of return will not keep up with inflation. In my opinion, whether we will have deflation or inflation is a political decision and thus is not predictable by reading current and past events. The government, of course, would prefer neither, but by its monetary and fiscal decisions, it will tilt the economy toward one or the other. Unfortunately, there is no longer room for any middle ground. We will either have deflation or inflation; therefore, the decision to buy or not buy bonds is like putting one's money on red or black when playing roulette.

Recommendations: For the time being, don't buy long-term bonds. At best, they should constitute only a small portion of your total investments. Buy bonds that have a short maturity. In particular, I recommend Treasury bills that mature in three or six months or in one year. Don't worry about losing a percent or two of interest. The most important thing is to preserve capital until the economy indicates whether it will be in a long-term inflationary or deflationary trend. It could be months, or years, before this trend becomes apparent. By holding Treasury bills you are not trying to outsmart or outguess anything; they will give you liquidity while saving you from the possible anguish of trying to figure out what is happening in the economy and discovering you were wrong. Bonds used to be promises to pay the holder a set amount of money. With the value of money subject to sudden change, it is a promise that cannot be kept.

As oil goes, so goes the economy.

In an economy that is changing rapidly, it is difficult to give investment advice that will be valid far into the future. Economic volatility and increasingly erratic government policies can overturn sound investment advice overnight. Most investment advisers, analysts, and newsletters assume that your decisions, at least in the stock and bond markets, concern which securities to buy or sell. In this last section, I mean to suggest a method whereby you can decide whether to be in the markets or not, whether to pull out, and, if so, when.

Throughout this book, I have written about the rising costs of energy, particularly oil. Oil has risen in ten years from $2.65 a barrel to $29, a 1,000 percent increase before accounting for inflation. Nevertheless, the price of oil could go down sharply in the next few years, and that could cause economic havoc. Does this contradict what I have been saying about the relationship among energy, labor, and capital? It does not. A drop in prices would correct the speculative rise that followed the Iranian revolution, but prices cannot return to the $3 per barrel that prevailed until 1973.

The world is in the midst of a deflationary period (see Chapter 4) in which the prices of virtually all commodities, with the exception of oil, are depressed. Those lower commodity prices have a punitive effect on the less-developed, debtor nations because these countries rely heavily, if not solely, on the export and sale of commodities for the income required to service their debts to foreign banks. Because the whole world has gone into a recession simultaneously (the last time this happened was in the 1930s), the demand for all commodities and products has also fallen at the same time, and this has pushed nations to the edge of bankruptcy. Argentina, for example, has demanded the unilateral rescheduling of its $34 billion in foreign debt. While the less-developed nations grapple with debts, some of the OPEC nations are also struggling, for the first time since 1974, to service their debts. In 1982, OPEC countries became net borrowers, taking more out of lending institutions than they were depositing from their oil revenues.

As global demand for oil has declined since 1979, primarily because of conservation efforts but also as a result of the worldwide recession, OPEC nations have had to cut back production from a high of 30 million barrels a day in 1979 to 19 million barrels in late 1982. In one year, from 1981 to 1982, Saudi Arabia cut production from 10 to 5.5 million barrels per day. Other countries have followed suit, but the OPEC agreement to cut production in order to maintain high prices is showing severe strain. As Mexico has already illustrated, nations that borrowed on their oil income must maintain certain levels of income or they cannot service their debts. Venezuela, Libya, Iraq, Nigeria, and Iran are all beginning to discount oil prices while upping production beyond the agreed-upon amounts. As they increase production in the face of stable or dropping demand, oil prices have become soft.

Shouldn't we be cheering? After all, conventional wisdom blames the "OPEC tax" for stalling Western economic growth during the 1970s; it further holds that if oil prices go down, a large portion of U.S. income that is now going to pay for oil can be directed back into consumption and investments, thus improving our prospects for economic growth. But we should not cheer. Ironically, it is the high price of oil that is propping up the world economy, preventing it from going into a full deflation.

If oil prices fall gently and slowly, such a drop will have a healthy effect on the world's economies. But if they should fall suddenly and sharply, financial chaos may result as some OPEC and non-OPEC nations scramble to find the extra income required to pay their debts. It is difficult to say what would happen if one or several nations defaulted on their debts to Western financial institutions.

Though the price of oil is a prop preventing full-scale deflation, there is no unanimity among OPEC nations about maintaining these prices. Venezuela's oil minister said in the fall of 1982 that OPEC needs to sell at least 25 million barrels a day to maintain its unity and financial health. If OPEC does not hold together as a functioning cartel, it would be easy to imagine a situation in which oil-producing countries ruthlessly cut prices in order to protect their market share and income—precisely the opposite behavior of that which brought the cartel into world power. Such an uncoordinated lowering of oil prices would lead to increased production as oil-producing nations tried to sell more oil for less money. But it could also lead to nations defaulting on their loans.

However, it is not only foreign producers who would be hurt by a disorderly retreat in prices: American and Canadian oil companies would also be severely affected. Many of them are financially vulnerable because they borrowed money to increase their oil exploration, development, and production based on their assumption—wrong, as it turns out—that prices would constantly rise. Even with the steadying of oil prices at $29 a barrel in the United States, there have been scores of bankruptcies by drillers, the near collapse of Dome Petroleum in Canada as well as the failure of Penn Square Bank, which had loaned heavily to oil concerns. Dupont and United States Steel recently completed mergers with Conoco and Marathon Oil, respectively, taking on multi-billion-dollar debts to finance these acquisitions. Any sharp reduction in oil prices could seriously threaten the ability of these industrial giants to stay in business in their present form.

Against this deflationary tension, the United States is in a process of "reliquifying" the economy. The Federal Reserve is relaxing its concern about the increase in monetary aggregates and is instead concentrating on lowering interest rates in order to stimulate the economy into another business cycle and recovery. The stock and bond markets have responded positively. From these actions, and given the unexpressed but pent-up demand in the economy, it is likely that the United States will stitch together an economic recovery between 1983 and 1985. It will take political will, which is already in evidence in Europe, the United States, and Japan, and it will take control over fiscal and monetary policies. The control over monetary policy is there, while fiscal policies, as reflected in the record projected U.S. budget deficits, are still out of control. Still, there is no reason why there can't be an economic recovery, though it would be anemic. As long as the reestablishment of liquidity in the American economy is achieved gradually, the economy should steadily grow. Inflation may again be the result, but only after two or three years have passed.

If any foreign nation was to walk away from its debts to American banks, the U.S. Federal Reserve Bank would have to become the "lender of last resort" and re-create the funds that had been lost. With such banks as Citibank, Bank of America, and Chase Manhattan having loaned substantially more than their capital and reserves to Latin America, substantial losses incurred by one or more of these banks would be made up by new funds from the Federal Reserve. The amount of money that would have to be loaned to the large banks in order to restore the confidence of Americans in their financial system would be so great that it could have the opposite effect—people would try to abandon the financial system by getting out of currency. While a runaway inflation would be possible in these circumstances, it is also possible that deflation could develop, because the injection of new liquidity might be too little too late. During the Depression, money was freely available at rock-bottom interest rates—2 to 3 percent—but nobody wanted to borrow. People had seen or suffered so many losses that even low interest rates could not entice them to borrow again.

Recommendations: Keep your attention on commodity prices. Markets, it is said, are there to fool you, not lead you. And the stock market, usually an accurate indicator of future growth, may deceive you if you do not also keep an eye on world oil prices. While it is true that there are some strong reasons for the Dow Jones to climb to 2,000 or more, such a run-up must be supported by changes in the marketplace for raw commodities. If there is a real worldwide economic recovery, the prices for commodities will rise, and oil should at least stabilize, if not go up. But if the stock market goes up without support from the commodities market, then I would pull out of the stock market and avoid it until there is confirmation. In terms of the marketplace, it is commodity prices that are going to determine what the economy does, not the stock market, because the world has lent itself trillions of dollars that can only be paid if the demand for and prices of those commodities rise. If they don't, the safest place for your money would be in short-term Treasury bills and Treasury bonds.

❋ Chapter 10

The Next
Economy

Both the U.S. and world economies are extremely complex, and no simple description or generalization can do them justice. Nevertheless, my purpose in describing the underlying structural changes in energy, capital, and labor is to provide you with an overall sense of how the economy is adjusting and evolving. Read that way, this book does not pretend to be an answer so much as a question: If these changes are occurring and will continue, what do they portend for the whole of the economy as well as its parts? How will they affect risk, productivity, family, government, culture, international relations, environment? Just as the impetus to conserve energy is restructuring our economy, so will a new economy restructure our society.

The informative economy is not necessarily a better one—it is only different. Just as the mass economy rather shone and glistened as we looked ahead toward more goods and prosperity, the informative economy may seem green and lush to some. However, a change of this magnitude has left and will continue to leave many people impoverished, confused, and unwilling to change. The informative economy is not a less materialistic economy than the mass economy—it is *more* materialistic. It is an economy in which material is given ever more scrutiny, in which matter, goods, and energy are highly valued and therefore more carefully controlled.

The decision on who controls the resources of modern civilization is a political one. The informative economy describes the structural form of the economy, but it does not describe its political bias. Compassion, understanding, and the willingness to deal with inequities do not emerge from the exchange of goods and services. It is an open question whether, having to be more careful about our use of natural resources, we will also be more careful about our human resource—one another.

How workers and business will respond to rapid economic restructuring is also unknown. Will labor and industry continue to blame other countries for their economic woes and to raise protective tariffs and restrictive trade barriers? Will we try to copy Britain's policy of "lemon" socialism, subsidizing our dying industries and smothering the new? Will we try to model ourselves after the Japanese and move toward greater cooperation between government and industry, aiming at economic growth and full employment? My guess is that in the end we will take the right course, but not, as Winston Churchill once mused, until we have tried everything else. The problems of Social Security, high budget deficits, record unemployment, and failing industries are either caused or aggravated by the decline of the mass economy. The temptation at the twilight of an industry to turn the clock back is overwhelming because it offers a false hope of quick relief. If we cannot see ahead to the economy that is trying to emerge, our economic policies will fail.

During the period of the mass economy, Americans sold Americans short. In general, big corporations saw the U.S. consumer as having large pockets and little discernment. One need only read the marketing studies done from the fifties through the seventies to understand how the mass economy perceived itself— as a group of people who were gullible and impulsive, susceptible to sex, glamour, and hyperbole. Perhaps we were. Certainly many of the businesses that operated on those assumptions were successful. But instead of looking at that period and behavior as indicators of an American character, it may be more plausible to conclude that the "gullibility" was a reaction to a sudden surge of wealth and prosperity that was difficult for the culture to digest all at once. Overnight we were, comparatively speaking, a society of the newly rich, with more than we knew how to use. This is not to suggest that Americans did not gain their wealth through work, sometimes even pluck and genius, but no one in 1946 could have foreseen the explosive increase in our national wealth that would take place over the next quarter-century. Like a big meal, it has been hard to digest. In the meantime, conditions have changed utterly. As we have seen, virtually every precondition of the "golden age of industrialism" has been reversed. If people who sold Jell-O and pink bathroom scales did well in the 1950s and 1960s, who will do well in the 1980s and 1990s?

First, those who do well will act on the assumption that Americans are intelligent and are becoming more so. Companies that try to fool their customers or manipulate their employees will find themselves, sooner or later, competitively threatened by a company that does no such thing. One of the underlying weaknesses of the U.S. auto industry has been its attitude toward customers and employees. Former General Motors chairman Thomas Murphy's statement that his company's purpose was "making money," not cars, still reverberates in the minds of consumers when pressed with a purchasing decision. That kind of sentiment puts not only employees at the bargaining table but consumers in an adversarial stance toward GM. If you manage a company, you hardly want either a customer or someone making your products as an adversary.

Although foreign cars had been in the American market for years, it was not until the Japanese invasion that Detroit was badly affected. Japan is a country that strives intensely to create labor harmony and customer satisfaction. Now that Detroit is starting to play catch-up with the Japanese, it is finding that it must redesign not only its cars, but the way in which it relates to its workers. W. Earl Sasser, a professor at Harvard Business School, has said, "The only way companies are going to solve problems like quality is by having functional cooperation." Industries not yet affected by such overt foreign competition might do well to study the auto industry and begin to change their manufacturing and marketing methods before they are forced to do so.

Second, those who do well will treat their customers and clients as they would themselves. In an increasingly sophisticated technological environment, people want to be compensated by having more human contact and social conviviality. Consumers are tired of two things: being treated as subordinates to a company, store, or institution and being seen as anonymous. People are looking for stores, service stations, hospitals, banks, and restaurants where they are treated as equals, as friends, and as trustworthy individuals: where, when a product goes wrong, they are treated not with suspicion, but with trust; where, when they forget their checkbook, they can send the check later;

where, when they need to have a product special-ordered, it is done with dispatch. The insensitive front is the weak point of mass merchandising. In a severe economic downturn, service will prove to be a powerful measure of who does well and who does not.

Third, and most important, those who do well in the informative economy will no longer make a distinction between how they act in the world and how they want to see the world act. Just as disintermediation is a trend toward the integration of production and distribution, owners, managers, and employees of companies must believe and embody the purpose, goal, or intent of their products or services. Why? Because these people and companies will naturally invest in their products the high component of informativeness required to succeed in coming years.

There may be no better example of such a company than Maytag, a maker of household appliances in Newton, Iowa. During the years 1980 and 1981, appliance sales dropped because of the recession and the slow-down in housing starts. Maytag, however, increased both its sales and market share during that time, selling products that were significantly more expensive than competing models. Maytag's ability to maintain stringent quality control has earned it a loyal clientele that seems to grow with each recession. If Maytag appears to be a prosaic example, its success points up the fact that what is being brought forth in the shift from a mass to an informative economy is not something new but something overlooked.

It would be nice to be able to take all the information presented so far and come up with a credo that would insulate one from economic travail: go long in gold, buy silver coins, leverage second-party real estate, store wheat, and so on. It would be simple—and wrong. The economy is a living system and includes within it our values. It is pointless to reduce its complexity to a set of speculations. The most important question during this economic transition is not what to do with our money, but what to do with our lives. To answer this question, we must have some idea how our individual and collective values will give rise to the next economy. One may double one's money by buying hard metals, but the gain will be insignificant compared with what one can earn and experience if one is able to redirect one's livelihood or business in such a way that it will flourish during the coming decades. This book cannot fully describe the informative economy because it is an economy still in the process of becoming. But between the simple ploys of survivalist thinking and the intricate machinations of macroeconomics, there are things to be done and changes to be aware of.

Instead of presenting a generalized list of recommendations for readers, I have written six letters, unsolicited, to different people representing different aspects of our society and economy. They are a retired person, a U.S. senator, a small-business person, a college student, a blue-collar worker, and the chairman of Exxon. By directly addressing the problems or ambitions of each of these people, I hope to show how to interpret and apply trends as they are outlined in the preceeding chapters; how the shift in the ratio of mass to information should concern Exxon and how the shift in the cost of capital should affect a retiree's planning. Each letter was written with an actual person in mind, but only Senator Cranston's and Chairman Garvin's real names are given.

Sarah is a second-year student at NYU, where she is torn between her love for theater and her desire to have an independent livelihood when she graduates. She does not intend to marry soon, and wants to sup-

*port herself even when she does. She is bright, but like
most nineteen-year-olds, she finds sitting for long hours
in front of her books an impossible distraction from
the heady life of New York City.*

Dear Sarah,

You, and I guess two million other college students,
are wondering whether you will find a good job when
you graduate—or even whether there will be an economy to find a job within. Twenty years ago my generation didn't seem to give much thought to life after
college, while today you hear hardly anything *but* talk
about professions. Indeed, as economic uncertainty
spreads, zeroing in on a profession seems the wisest
course. Whoever heard of a depression for doctors or
bankers? But this rush to professions, coined the "proto-
professional compulsion" by James Ogilvy, may be the
worst approach to take to education in a time of economic uncertainty.

Although it is certainly not a view that is widely
shared, I believe that within the next decade we will
see a change in our economic fortunes, both for the
better and for the worse. To understand this, you should
distinguish monetary problems from economic problems. The U.S. economy depends on growth for its
well-being. What the headlines are reflecting is what
happens when the economy doesn't grow: deficits, high
interest rates, inflation, joblessness, bankruptcies, and
bank failures. The news is frightening, and during the
past ten years the economy has been getting worse.
There are powerful reasons for this slowing of economic growth, but the most important is that the very
nature of our industrial, "mass" economy has caused
it to reach some very real limits in terms of what the
environment can provide and support. Since it is our
economy, and our planet, we are on both sides of the
conflict. We can only win *and* lose. What are we going
to lose? Not the economy, because economies do not

disappear. They do reach certain points where they change, and during those transitions everything seems unsettled and up for grabs. What we might lose instead is our monetary system, the standard of our currency that the government backs with its "full faith and credit." As the economy has weakened over the past decade, we have thrown money at it relentlessly; we have lowered taxes and then raised them, gone deeply into debt, raised federal deficits to historic levels, and weakened our entire monetary system to the point where even the failure of the smallest bank sends tremors through the system. There is, unfortunately, little that you and I can do about the monetary system. But there is much we can do in terms of the economy, because we create it daily.

If I could recommend a single book on the economy that might lift the veil of our economic crises, it would be Fernand Braudel's *Structures of Everyday Life*. Braudel, at seventy-nine, stated the problem succinctly in a recent interview: "The crisis is at the top, not at the bottom." He cites Italy as an example of a country torn by crises, chaos, terrorism, strikes, inflation, and governmental breakdown. And yet, throughout Italy, people work, make money, and have families. They learn, play, and die. And the reason for this, according to Braudel, is that there are three economic layers rather than one. The bottom layer, "everyday life," is the material layer of daily work: making bread, cleaning clothes, catching fish, and disposing of the debris. Above that is the market economy layer of buying and selling. Above that is the layer of banks, large companies, and governments. This last layer is the world we read about, the world that is in crisis because, according to Braudel, it depends on manipulating people in the lower levels who are no longer willing to be manipulated. In my book, I have described the end of the mass economy, which in many ways parallels this top layer, and the rise of an informative economy, which is how the bottom layers are changing.

The worst approach to these crises is to choose a conservative profession, a sort of vocational heading-for-the-hills. It may seem safe and sure, but is hardly the kind of training that will prepare you for the future. If anything, it prepares you for the past, because the economy and the world are changing too fast. The economy is fragmenting completely. We will no longer have one or even three economies. There will be dozens, intertwined and interacting.

One of the economic changes will be the shift in sovereignty over capital, which simply means that people will take charge of their money. No longer will they entrust it to banks; instead, they will move it around, causing the financial markets and interest rates to remain volatile. Second, the so-called underground economy will continue to grow and even burgeon over the next decades. There will be a roiling cash culture of swap meets, barter, and bootlegging (marijuana). Third, there will be tremendous polarization. The rich will become richer and more outrageous than ever. We are a terribly wealthy country, and the rich here won't let us forget it. In consumer markets, there will be at least three tiers. In clothing, for example, the first tier will be expensive, designer clothes of impeccable quality and workmanship sold at mythical prices. The second tier, "investment clothing," will not go out of fashion, will last for a long time, and will be bought by the vast middle and upper-middle class. They will have to buy this way as their incomes slowly decline. Then, there will be the heavy discounters selling utility clothing, remainders, and closeouts at rock-bottom prices. Most everything else in between will have a tough time. We will see this in many markets, from autos to food.

Another trend will be what banker Alan Rothenberg, president of the London & San Francisco Co., Ltd., calls the "Electronic Protestant." The handling of money will be so totally computerized that you will no longer have to sit in front of Mr. Bottomly at the bank and wring your hands while explaining why you want to borrow $2,500 to build a darkroom in your garage. Banking will be done by computers that will assess your balance sheet and decide whether to give you the money. This fiscal reformation will mean you can borrow the money for anything—no one will care why.

Another trend: Goods and services will be delivered through more disintermediated channels, and I define disintermediation as the elimination of middlemen and other intermediary people, processes, and functions. Your medical and dental records will be on computer floppy discs, for example, and the discs will be in your possession. You will consult by telephone medical practitioners who will be able to update your medical record in your home computer. Again, the sovereignty will change—from doctor to patient. You will buy bread directly from bakeries, clothes from tailors, dishes from potteries, and generate energy from photo-voltaics. In other words, you will see the production of goods more closely integrated with their distribution and sale. Large corporations will change from producers to distributors. Utilities will buy back your overflow electricity; authors will become venture capitalists by investing in their own books rather than taking advances, and the publishers will make their money on distribution. TV networks will all own large cable systems and become more concerned with program distribution than generation.

Despite the present economic unwinding, we are on the verge of enormous and revolutionary technological changes. Soon we will have ceramic engine blocks in cars that will get 120 miles per gallon. There will be an exponential increase in our ability to generate and transmit information through computers; not knowing and learning about computers will be like living in Los Angeles and not learning how to drive. There will be new materials, new industries, new livelihoods, and, apparently, new organisms. Not all technologies will prove beneficial, but that has always been the case. So whatever degree you take, it should include the widest possible curriculum, from Greek to cybernetics, from molecular biology to drama.

I understand that you are considering a master's degree in business administration. I would caution you to design your own educational format rather than reach for one that is essentially a credential. A credential allows other people with credentials to accept you more easily, but your innate curiosity requires more than diplomas. I once was asked to speak to a graduating class of MBAs, supposedly because I was an entrepreneur and had made a go of it. The class was raring to get out and become entrepreneurs. While I couldn't help but wish that I had had their academic knowledge of accounting, banking, financing, and marketing when I stumbled into business some seventeen years ago, I told them that now that they were leaving their institution they had to forget most of what they'd learned. When reading stories about many successful people in different fields—scientists, businesspersons, inventors—I have been struck by how many of them were essentially naïve in many ways and, therefore, looked at problems with fresh, unprofessional eyes. When Buckminster Fuller was in the navy, he asked himself why the bubbles in a boat's wake were round. This might sound like a "dumb" question, but it led him to geodesic domes and hundreds of other discoveries.

If you do take your master's in business administration, always remember that the economy is the relationship between living beings and the earth—another living "being." Don't be fooled into thinking that the economy is merely the study of the production and distribution of goods and services, because as soon as you see the economy as inanimate, you begin to think in manipulative ways. And as soon as you begin to try to manipulate, you have nowhere to go but to the top layer, where credentials are sacred and crises endemic. (James Ogilvy called professional specialization the "cash cropping of human resources.") Don't be misled by external definitions of what your potential is as you acquire your education. Make up your own definitions, and when you leave, pursue the field you love most. In the end that is the field that will reward you best. The next economy will be led by those who are the most intelligent in their field. This intelligence will not be a measure of IQ, but a measure of how thoroughly our lives and work are integrated.

Sincerely,
Paul Hawken

Senator Alan Cranston is the senior senator from the state of California, the most populous and wealthy state in the union. As Californians are often told by their elected representatives, California would be the eighth largest country in the world if it were a separate political entity. Not surprisingly, it has been a postwar tradition for California officials to aspire to the White House: witness Richard Nixon, Ronald Reagan, and the thus far unsuccessful Jerry Brown. Senator Cranston has declared that he will be a candidate in the 1984 presidential campaign.

Senator Alan Cranston
Washington, D.C.

Dear Senator Cranston:
As the senior senator from California, you will no doubt be required to address the issue of the budget in the Senate as well as during your presidential campaign in 1983. You have held your Senate seat by consistently uniting the traditional Democratic blocks of labor, blacks, the elderly, Hispanics, Jews, and a solid plurality of the middle class. Since, as a Democrat, you

have been largely responsible, along with your colleagues, for the overall increase in welfare, Social Security, and Medicare programs passed by Congress over the past decade and since you do not propose cutting Social Security benefits to recipients, I would like to know how you intend to balance the budget if you are elected President, or if you remain a senator.

As you know, part of the reason Social Security benefits became so politicized was Wilbur Mills's political aspirations. Prior to his 1972 bid for the presidency, Mills (chairman of the House Ways and Means Committee) rammed through a 20 percent increase in benefits. A year later the Republicans, trying to "depoliticize" Social Security, initiated a measure that indexed benefits. A year after that we had OPEC and double-digit inflation, and the rest is history. Nearly 50 percent of today's budget is transfer payments. When speaking privately, you recognize better than anyone how close we have come to bankrupting the system. And as a politician, you know what you have to say to get elected. The question is: How are you going to bring these two "realities" closer together? The second biggest budget item is defense and the third is the interest payments on the national debt. Defense can be cut significantly, but by itself this would not come close to reducing the government's $200 billion deficit. What's left? Transfer payments, and the largest of these is Social Security.

Since 1973, this country has been on a new economic course but neither the Senate nor Congress has seen the direction clearly. In 1973, because of the surge in oil prices, the mass economy, which was the underlying structure of the industrial age, began to contract and make room for the new "informative" economy. The fact that oil prices went up is not in itself so important. What was striking about that period and the decade that followed was the reversal of the critical relation between the cost of energy and the cost of labor. Until then labor had been going up in value and energy down. Since then it has been the opposite, so that today we have the same relationship between energy and labor that prevailed in 1910. This fact has tremendous implications for you and anyone else trying to create an intelligent fiscal policy and balance the budget.

Because labor has been going down (real wages have declined 16 percent in ten years, while the price of energy has climbed 500 percent), we will see, albeit slowly, a gradual ebbing of the consumer society. People don't have the same income they once had—how could they with double-digit inflation and the lowered productivity brought on by rising energy costs?

I find it extraordinary that Ronald Reagan would forfeit one of the greatest political mandates given a President in this century. There is no question but that voters gave him permission to reduce the size of government, to slow its rate of growth, and balance the budget. Had I been he, rather than trying to balance the budget piecemeal by chopping here and there, I would have gone on television and said, "There is no fair way to cut the budget and not hurt someone, some group, or interest. So instead of fighting it out, let's cut 15 percent from every program, department, and entitlement. And when the budget is balanced, we can examine how to rearrange fiscal priorities according to the will of the people." How could anyone have opposed that? We would have felt united behind such a fair policy, that we were doing something together, as a nation, and that the belt tightening was a shared condition. But instead Reagan spent more.

As I see it, you and your colleagues in the House and Senate now have three choices. First, the House can follow the historical route of raising taxes and smothering the economy. That route has failed before and there is no reason why it can't fail again. Try to find a dentist in Australia on a Friday. They're all home or fishing because by the fifth day of the week they would rather have the free time than pay the high marginal tax rates.

The second choice is to do nothing, loudly. This appears to be what we are doing now. First we lower taxes, then we raise them, expand defense spending and chop welfare, and leave the untouchables like Social Security alone. But when all is said and done, government spending under Reagan is exactly the same or higher as a percentage of GNP than it was under Carter; the rich have more, the poor have less, and deficits continue to grow.

The third choice is the Margaret Thatcher "let them eat cake" policy, where the government clamps down on the monetary supply, creates high unemployment, lowered revenues, increased deficits, and tighter monetary policy to control the inflation caused by the increased deficits.

I would like to suggest a fourth way.

Simply speaking, we are living above our means. The deficit is not some mysterious malady that defies diagnosis. It is exactly the same gap between income and expenditures that you or I experience when we spend more than we earn. The difference is that as individuals we will suffer immediate repercussions. Our credit cards will be invalidated or our checking accounts closed. When the government overspends, it does not suffer itself, but, instead, the world feels the repercussions in the form of inflation, high interest rates, and economic dislocation. As a Democrat, you, and the people who elected you, feel that most of what we are spending our money on is truly necessary. In other words, with the possible exception of Pentagon excesses, spending 34 percent of our GNP on government is acceptable. (Germany spends 48 percent.)

That being the case, the question is how to raise revenues. The way sought by Democrats and Republicans alike is economic growth. It is the "if only" plan—if only interest rates would fall, capital spending increase, housing starts go up, and consumers buy cars. This plan has two flaws. First, the economy hasn't grown, and second, even if it does, the present fiscal policy would create deficits right through the nineties.

Instead, tax oil. Why oil? The government can tax *four* basic areas. It can tax labor—wages—and does. It can tax business, and does. It can tax consumption in the form of sales taxes, excise taxes, duties and luxury taxes, as well as taxes on energy. It can tax capital, and does, through capital-gains taxes. In the case of labor and business, further taxes may depress economic activity and further weaken the economy. Taxing most consumption items, through a European-style value added tax, discriminates in favor of the wealthy (to whom taxes are hardly more than a nuisance), and also suppresses spending and economic activity. Taxing oil, however, has a curious effect.

It is the rise in the price of oil that has caused much of the economic dislocation we have experienced for the past decade and that has caused the decline in labor productivity and incomes. Why make oil more expensive? The cost of oil is going to go up anyway over the next few decades. And as it does, it will bring about structural changes in the economy that are healthy in three ways. First, it will reduce energy consumption, which will lower the amount of oil imported from other countries. Second, it will create incentives in every home and industry to conserve and become efficient, and this will become a powerful economic force to create energy-conservation industries in the United States. Third, by helping balance the budget, moneys now loaned to the government can be freed for true economic growth.

At this writing, the government is consuming over 70 percent of all personal and business savings to feed its continually growing deficits. With that money available to business at markedly lower interest rates, we would have sufficient capital to begin concentrating on innovative technologies, real productive gains, and new capital spending.

Oil is the linchpin of this economy. Taxing it will make it even more critical. It is the only tax I know of that makes what is being taxed more valuable. When you tax labor too highly (as is being done with the new Social Security taxes), business eliminates workers. When you tax energy, it becomes more precious. And as it becomes more precious, we find ways to use it more wisely. The kind of tax I am talking about is a big one: $1 per gallon at retail. Before people object vociferously, they might ask how Switzerland, with no oil resources, can pay such a tax and have a per capita income 50 percent greater than our own.

The initiation of such a tax would be painful, but not as painful as reduced Social Security benefits, high interest rates, or a collapsing economy. If America raised the price of oil by such a margin, it is my belief that we would quickly become world leaders in all phases of energy conservation and alternative energy generation.

Energy, then, is both our bane and boon. If we let ourselves be hammered by erratic price increases, our economy will experience the lurching "slowth" that has become so painful. But if instead we accept the message of those price increases and look ahead, we will rediscover our society's greatest resources—ingenuity, technical innovation, and flexibility in the face of adversity. By taxing energy we will speed up the shift from the mass economy to the informative economy, or, to put it slightly differently, the shift in ratio of mass to information in our production methods and our goods. When mass (energy, in this case) becomes too expensive, intelligence comes to the fore.

As the senator from the most technologically innovative state in the Union, you must surely recognize that in order to maintain our leadership, we need both the capital to invest and the incentives. A tax on energy, as contradictory as it sounds on the surface, can provide America with the incentive to lead the world in energy development and conservation at an accelerated pace. Remember, energy is, and will be for the foreseeable future, the largest business in the world.

Sincerely,
Paul Hawken

David has bought an old-fashioned hardware store in New Hampshire. On the outskirts of town, there is a new building-supply store that is part of a large, nationwide chain. It has 60,000 square feet of display and a 10-acre parking lot. David's store is small, compact, and still has wooden drawers for storing screws and bolts in bulk rather than on cards on pegboard. The previous owner, who retired, was losing business rapidly to the new chain. David thought he could make the store into a profitable business again, and so far he is holding his own.

Dear David,
Starting a small business is definitely a gutsy and perilous economic activity. No single exercise puts your money, livelihood, and self-esteem on the line more directly. For some the exercise is fulfilling, while for others it can be a complete financial and emotional disaster. What is the critical difference between a business that succeeds and one that fails?

Although many factors contribute to a successful business—financing, location, management, and good accounting, to name a few—I'd like to talk about one that is seldom mentioned: why someone shops at a small business rather than a large one. After all, in most cases, large businesses have better selection and lower prices. The critical difference between success and failure, I think, can be summed up in the word *information*. Let me give you an example.

I have some student friends who own and operate a small grocery store in a San Francisco ghetto not six blocks from a Safeway store. Their store is only 700 square feet, yet from all points of view it is a success. Customers like it, it is fun to work in, and it is profitable. The store previously had been a mom-and-pop operation of the sort that used to dot many corners of San Francisco. The previous owner was killed by an assailant, and before that the store had been robbed three times in one year. It was boarded up and derelict when my friends bought the site. Conventional wisdom would suggest that between the local Safeway, with its low prices and vast selection, and the danger of operating a small store in a high-crime area, opening the business was a bad decision. But what my student friends did (though I'm sure they would not use my term) was to change the ratio between mass and information in their store. They created an information-rich environment that offered both quality and economy.

There are five key ways in which they did this.

First, the store is located in an area populated by blacks, gays, senior citizens, whites, and students. It is a dangerous neighborhood at night, and sometimes in the day. The first decision they made was to "open up" the store. Because the neighborhood was so dangerous, the previous owner had put steel mesh over the windows, which had been plastered with beer and liquor posters. It was impossible to see into the store from the street, and inside it felt like being in an armory. By removing the steel mesh and all the signs, and by enlarging the windows, the owners made the interior of the store visible from halfway up the block. Robbers would feel exposed now, so the store is no longer a likely target.

Second, the people who were robbing the store were doing so, in part, and perhaps unconsciously, because the store made all its money from liquor, and neighborhood people felt taken advantage of because of the high prices. The previous owners had not lived nearby. My friends decided for personal reasons, and because it seemed to draw unsavory types, not to sell any alcohol.

Third, they became discerning buyers, showing up early in the morning at produce markets, getting to know all the vendors, and discovering bargains that were available at the end of the vending day when brokers and farmers wanted to clean out their stock. Being small, they could buy cases of avocados or flats of peaches at low prices, take good markups, and still undersell Safeway.

Fourth, because they have limited floor space, they don't try to carry everything. Their clientele reflects a broad mix of tastes, from ethnic to health to gourmet. Their stock is highly eclectic, with items from Coke to turnip greens, from yogurt to croissants, but it concentrates mainly on fresh, low-priced produce—something that everyone wants. On such key items as milk and bread, they meet the loss-leading prices of Safeway. In fact, market-based tests have shown this store is cheaper than Safeway, though markups are higher. Another area where they make better markups is in cheeses. Again, because of their size, they can buy slightly damaged rounds from importers, cut out the bad spots, and wrap up the rest for customers at prices 25 percent lower than other stores.

Fifth, they love their work, know their products intimately, and can speak intelligently to customers about what they are selling, current produce prices, and quality in general. They are now large enough to have some buying clout with suppliers but still small enough to handle special orders and requests. In other words, they satisfy the needs of their surrounding community by being both more labor- and information-intensive. They spend more time informing customers about their products and more time learning about what they sell than their competition does.

Implementing these five steps has resulted in a 10 percent profit margin, virtually unheard of in the grocery business.

Because you are opening a small hardware store, some of this may not seem applicable. But what is pertinent is this sense of informativeness—that is, the creation of an information-rich environment. My thesis is that all customers are intelligent, but many are ignorant: they probably don't know much about what they are buying but are avid learners if given the right information. Most people are too shy to admit this, and most stores are too intimidating to allow people to admit it.

If I were you, I would not try to compete on high-volume, low-margin items such as Sheetrock and two-by-fours. Leave that to the chain store down the road. Like the grocery store, don't try to have one of everything, because you can't afford it. Concentrate instead on finding those products that are much needed and are best in quality. Every product area has a range from the awful to the elite. Your customers don't want the awful and they can't afford the elite. Use your connections and knowledge as a former builder to find and sell those items that are both of high quality and reasonably priced. They are, after all, the tools you bought and the hardware you put in the houses you built. You know these lines. A customer prefers a store with a limited selection of brands, staffed by people who know their inventory thoroughly, to a big inventory attended by ignorant clerks. Sell only those items you believe in and can fully back. Even if they are more expensive than nationally advertised brands and not as well known, your customers will respect your knowledge more than the incessant commercials they see during football games. Most people who own homes have already been through the early stages when they had to buy cheap screwdrivers and appliances. They have seen them fall apart. Now they want things that will last and are willing to pay the extra premium to a store that can offer that assurance.

Another friend has in his store this quote from John Ruskin: "The common law of business balance prohibits paying a little and getting a lot—it can't be done. If you deal with the lowest bidder, it is well to add something for the risk you run and if you do that you'll have enough for something better." Americans are learning that lesson, and the huge chains cannot supply them with their needs. These stores depend on enormous volume and do business on a "sell anything to anyone" philosophy. They may make it with that philosophy, but a small business cannot. The main thing to remember is that you are a service, and that the products you sell are the means for providing that service, which is the knowledge, care, and attention that you and your staff can offer. If you keep that in mind, you will never have to worry about failing as a small businessman. In fact, you may surprise everyone by becoming a big one, if you're not careful.

With kindest regards,
Paul

Clifton C. Garvin, Jr., is the chairman of Exxon, the world's largest corporation, with assets of $62 billion; yearly sales in 1981 were $108 billion, and profits were $5.5 billion. The corporation owns or operates over

500 ships, 62 refineries, 13,000 oil wells, and 66,000 gas stations under the Esso or Exxon brand and employs 180,000 people.

Clifton C. Garvin, Jr., Chairman
Exxon Corporation
Rockefeller Center
New York, New York

Dear Mr. Garvin,

Since you are a busy man, I will try to get right to the point. Don't be fooled by your size. As chairman of the world's largest company your most difficult task is to plan for the future. Because your main business is oil, planning is all the more complex. Decisions made now could end up years later costing or making the company many billions of dollars.

From its beginnings in 1870 as Standard Oil, Exxon, in its growth and development, has paralleled the age of industrialism. If the original Standard Oil trust had not been broken up by the Supreme Court in 1911, Standard Oil's revenues would today equal the GNP of England or China, a testimony to the importance that oil has played in industrialization. As it is, your revenues equal the GNP of Sweden.

Because Exxon for so long has been able to count on its engineers to find oil and to count on the world to consume it in ever-larger amounts, your corporation's emphasis has been on extraction and development. While this activity will remain critically important to a healthy oil company, the past growth of oil consumption will not occur again, and Exxon can no longer rely on a seller's market. As oil production is increasingly nationalized in the Third World, Exxon's role will shift to marketing, a difficult area for a company long managed by engineers.

Almost everything you have done *outside* the oil business has failed in two significant ways. First, it has not contributed to the strength and growth of Exxon. Second, it has diverted resources and capital away from what you do well and so has helped neither you nor the public. You have racked up millions of dollars of losses in these outside businesses, ranging from mining to office equipment to electric motors.

Because you are a big business you are trapped by doing things in large ways. But it is one thing to start a business that becomes large and entirely another to start things on a large scale. You should imitate nature, where meaningful beginnings are almost unnoticeable. I suspect no one could have predicted that the commodity firm of Clark & Rockefeller would lead to the world's largest company. The world doesn't need another massive project or mine. It needs intelligent development, which means that your future businesses will require sensitivity to people, place, and time. Royal Dutch/Shell, your largest competitor and the second largest company in the world, several years ago instituted a practice of filing "social impact reports" before funding a new refinery or plant. The purpose of the reports was to measure the impact Shell's investment would have on the local society as well as how Shell would be perceived by the region. Projects that looked as though they would meet a negative reception were canceled even if they were "economical" on paper.

It is difficult for you to perceive the impact Exxon makes on the world, since your very size inhibits such perception. It is as if you wear eyeglasses that make everything large and gross, glasses that eliminate the minute, the detailed, and the seemingly inconsequential. This perception will have to change if Exxon is to grow, not merely in size but in a healthy manner—in other words, *develop*. It is this faulty perception that caused Exxon to buy Reliance Electric for $1.24 billion, an investment analysts say you will never recoup. You have gone into mining in a big way, losing over $500 million so far. You bought a string of office-equipment companies and then watched many of the creative people in those companies walk away from you to start again with smaller companies. Did you, when you purchased Qyx, Qwip, and Vydec, study what impact your purchase would have on personnel?

Unlike some of my peers, I am not against size per se. But because of your scale and because the industrial world as it is presently constituted has peaked, Exxon must radically change its strategy in order to fill both its own need for internal development and the world economy's need for intelligent restructuring. The main problem with Exxon is this: people do not feel that you are there to help. You may object to that judgment and point to how Exxon is actively spending its capital to find and develop new supplies of energy, but the perception remains and it will not be changed by capital spending. I think the perception is largely accurate. You yourself told shareholders in 1978 that "public attitude[s] towards the company ... are quite negative." This negative perception is becoming significant not only to society but to your employees as well. Like most large companies, Exxon can put out internal reports full of smiling faces and good works, but the perception of how well you are supposedly doing on the inside must in some way square with how people think on the outside. *Neurosis* has been defined as "having a perception of self that is widely divergent from how others see you." Using that definition, Exxon may be neurotic.

Let me be specific. The oil business has completely changed over the past ten years. Exxon used to make its money by finding oil. Its refining and marketing system was the means to obtain revenues but not really profits. Profits were in the ground. With the rise of OPEC and the nationalization of ARAMCO and your assets in Saudi Arabia, you and other oil giants have increasingly come to rely on the "downstream" activities of refining and retailing for your profits. This strategy worked, especially during the two oil shortages in this country. But now we face a period of overcapacity in which consumption is falling in industrialized countries and there are too many refineries. Even as oil goes up in price, most of the increase will be absorbed by OPEC, not Exxon. Thus oil has come to resemble a commodity business, and profits depend more and more on marketing. This means that Exxon should look carefully at what could be its Achilles heel, marketing, or, more specifically, its service stations.

Because the industrial economy has peaked, growth in petroleum sales will be rather limited. Consequently many existing retail outlets for gasoline will close as they begin to incur losses for their parent companies. For example, Mobil announced in fall 1982 that it was closing a thousand stations and you announced the closing of 850 of your own. In order to make your existing stations more valuable to you and to others, you must change what I call the ratio between "mass and information," the emphasis that is placed on the product of the business (in your case, oil) and the information of the business (service). I cannot think of a retail business in all of the United States that asks less training and less employee awareness than gas stations. There is, not far from where I work, an Exxon station. And with all due respect, the people who are employed there are some of the rudest characters you'll ever want to meet. I am sure that if you used this station you would be furious that your name is on it. But your name *is* on it, and on 66,000 other service stations worldwide.

When there are fuel shortages we will get gas where we can. But the rest of the time we continue to try to find real people behind our gas pumps, not corporate blandishment. And although this is not a critical problem now, you should look at it before it becomes one. As gasoline consumption in the United States continues to fall over the next decade, many more gas stations will become marginal and close. Exxon, with its vast resources, can keep its open, but will lose money doing so. It would be far better to take a new look at the meaning of gas retailing. The company that can establish a truly consistent and first-rate level of service will find that customers go out of their way to patronize its stations. It is said that it is impossible to provide good service in the low-margin business of gasoline retailing, but I would point to another low-margin business: hamburgers. Whatever your opinion of McDonald's hamburgers, the company has developed a consistent and productive degree of service throughout its 5,000 outlets even though most are not company-owned but franchised. Having knowledgeable, friendly people at a gas pump is going to make the difference in the retailing end of the oil business over the coming decades. With over $5 billion in profits and perhaps twice that in cash flow, Exxon certainly has the revenues and the incentive to train and develop that end of the business. As for the mining, motors, and office-equipment companies, I would sell them. The very fact that the only place you could expand is into areas outside your expertise means that you have a policy of growth for the sake of growth. In the shift from the mass economy of the industrialized age to the emerging informative economy, the key will be development, not growth. If Exxon develops what it currently has, it will grow well enough. If it merely tries to grow, it may neither develop nor grow and may find it is wasting both its money and its time.

Sincerely,
Paul Hawken

Mrs. Robertson is sixty years old, lives by herself, and is retired. Her only income is a disability payment from a job-related injury suffered ten years ago. She supplements her income by raising specialty birds such as the Chinese button quail. Her assets consist almost *entirely of savings. She is frugal and spends no more than $8,000 per year to support herself. Despite her modest means, she is managing to save money every year.*

Dear Mrs. Robertson,

I know that you are wondering, with all the news about soaring stock prices and failing banks, if your money and, indeed, if your future are secure. Or, to put it another way, it seems that the barrage of economic news means that all of us should do something with our money rather than just sit like ducks in a pond. But in your case, being a duck is the best thing.

When I suggested that you sell your home in 1979, you had serious doubts. After all, prices were rising quickly and the house represented your largest financial asset. It was practically paid for. At any rate you sold it for $59,000 and, after expenses, were able to put $46,000 in the bank. That together with your other savings gave you about $60,000 in cash, all of which is either in government-denominated money-market funds or in Treasury bills. Since you sold that house, you have reinvested the earnings from these savings and have gained another $18,000 from interest paid, which is approximately the same amount your house has appreciated since then. The difference is that when you sold your house you were able to get all cash. The people who are now selling houses in that price range are having to take back second or third mortgages as well as lower their asking prices. Not only are prices soft, but the buyers are barely able to make the payments and feel strapped for cash. I would rather you had a Treasury bill than a third mortgage. Furthermore, the property was too much for you to take care of, and the rent on the house you are now paying allows you to live closer to your grandchildren, though it doesn't increase your monthly expenses much beyond what they were when you were a homeowner.

As to your capital, I have urged you to keep it in Capital Preservation I, a money-market fund that only buys government securities and does not deal in "repos." Repos are repurchase agreements that are bought and sold by securities firms, brokers, and banks; these agreements say that a firm will deliver a security at a given date and pay a given interest rate. Originally these were used as a means to give liquidity to the financial system, so that instead of transferring ownership of securities or borrowing on them, firms sold chits that represented the securities. This sounds fine, but we saw in the collapse of Drysdale Securities a case of a firm speculating on interest rates and getting caught with huge losses that it could not cover. When it came time to repay Chase Manhattan, the agent to whom Drysdale sold their repos, they could not. Chase had to write off over $210 million because a few guys in the back rooms of Drysdale made a wrong decision. A few weeks later another government securities firm, Lombard-Wall, also defaulted. Therefore, to avoid the remote, but real, possibility of the loss of your savings, I think you are better off with Capital Preservation.

It is amazing that the world economy has become so complicated and perilous that I cannot tell you to put your money in a large bank and forget about it. But it seems that those who are forgetting about money now *are* the large banks, which means that you had better pay close attention to it. The world financial system has become as fragile as a swallow's egg. Many large banks are nearly bankrupt, with nonpaying loans far exceeding their capital and reserves. Imagine that someone owes you $100,000. When it comes time to pay, the person says that not only can he not pay you but that he will have to borrow the interest. So you lend him $10,000 for interest. How long would you continue to do that and still call that loan an asset? That is the dilemma that faces Western banks that have given Third World countries enough fiscal rope with which to hang themselves. Mexico and Brazil owe banks over $175 billion, while smaller countries like Poland and Argentina owe $27 billion and $34 billion respectively. Thirty-four countries have told us that they cannot pay their debts and will need even *more* money from us. (The United States loaned $5 billion more to Mexico toward the end of 1982.)

You have lived just long enough to have witnessed the domino effect of the bank failures between 1930 and 1934. People like you who worked hard all their lives lost everything because of someone else's stupidity and greed. I hope that those who say it can't happen again are right, but I would prefer that you found out while holding T-bills rather than a bank deposit.

Right now it may look foolish to save and earn only interest, especially when there seem to be a hundred schemes to earn more than simple interest. But the 1980s will differ from the past decade, and people who save will do well indeed. Stories of pensioners losing their retirement funds in savings banks because of the erosive effects of inflation were certainly true during the 1970s, but there is now simply too much debt on the one hand, and too much sophistication among small savers and investors on the other, to allow that to happen again. I think deflation is an event likely to occur over the next few years. But even if inflation accelerates again, interest rates will more than keep up with it because, unlike the seventies, when people were unprepared, everyone from institutions to small savers will demand what is called the inflation premium. We will not see negative interest rates again, as we did in 1978–79, when one could borrow money at rates lower than the rate of inflation. The economy is getting to be such a rough place that I can't think of a better personal stance for you than to be one of the many lenders to the federal

government. Keep rolling over the Treasury bills and
adding to your Capital Preservation account so that
you can concentrate on the things you love, like raising
button quail and playing with your grandchildren.

Sincerely,
Paul Hawken

*Franklin Jefferson is a forty-seven-year-old machinist
working at Precision Fabrication in Flint, Michigan.
It is one of the primary producers of brake and wheel
hubs for the local Buick plant. In the past three years,
Precision has laid off half its work force, including
Franklin's brother-in-law. More layoffs are rumored.*

Dear Franklin,
No one can say at this point whether the automobile
industry has hit bottom and will recover or whether it
is just pausing before another decline. I suspect it might
be both—that we might see a recovery in 1983–84 but
an even sharper reduction in the production of domestic automobiles by mid-decade.

To figure out what to do now, it is necessary to
backtrack a little. The U.S. automobile industry came
out of World War II with good plant capacity, lots of
ex-soldiers ready to work and buy cars, and with a
record amount of pent-up savings from the war to back
up those desires. For almost thirty years after the war,
the industry was blessed by a combination of circumstances that will never be repeated. Fuel prices dropped
by half between 1945 and 1970, real wages doubled
during the same period, and technological efficiencies
kept reducing the amount of labor required to make a
car. When those factors combined with the subsequent
buying surge of the post-war-baby-boom children, now
grown up, in the late sixties and early seventies, the
industry flourished. Year after year from about 1947
until 1973, cars were getting cheaper to buy. As cars

got cheaper, demand expanded, production increased, and the industry grew.

During this time, cars were bought and made for show. Every fall, cars completely changed in appearance. We weren't just buying transportation, we were making a statement. And car makers obliged with literally hundreds of models, options, colors, and body styles. What was lost in the shuffle was quality. And why not? Americans could turn over their "rolling stock" every few years, so cars didn't need to last ten or twenty years. Furthermore, few people wanted to make that kind of investment, since five years later cars were actually cheaper when compared with increases in income.

In this same period, the United Auto Workers asked for generous pay and benefits from the industry. Profits were high, and workers rightly demanded their fair share and got it. Despite the strikes, disputes, and antagonisms that built up in the industry, it was a win-win situation for both sides. The American auto worker became the highest paid in the world, and the American auto industry became the largest and most profitable in the world. What went wrong?

In one sense, nothing has gone wrong. But the conditions of cheap fuel and rising wages have completely reversed, and the industry, heady with its own success, was blind-sided by its own ignorance of the change. There were lots of signs: the rising number of imports during the sixties, especially in college towns, and books and articles attacking the industry for its planned obsolescence, waste, and consumer manipulation. But these were shrugged off. Now the industry, hard hit by Japanese and European competition, is scrambling to catch up. But change has been late in coming. To use different economic parlance, the industry was built up on having a high ratio of mass to a low amount of information. Lots of mass because cars were big and heavy, gulped fuel, and were not made to be here very long. Low in information because the emphasis on volume and model shifts meant quality, durability, and ease of maintenance were given low priority.

Now contrast the American auto industry with those of Japan and Europe. These countries were devastated by the war. They came out with no savings, low incomes, and governments that placed high taxes on fuel to support their efforts at reconstruction and social welfare. They made cars that were tiny, sipped fuel, and used much less material than ours. We laughed at them. They were second-rate. And they were—at first. But while we were basking in success, they kept improving their cars, making them more durable, efficient, and economical to produce and own. In other words, because they could not afford the extra mass—larger, heavier cars that used more fuel—they concentrated on information—engineering, technological innovation, quality, materials, and design.

Since oil prices rose in 1973–74, our economy more and more has taken on the appearance of theirs after the war: wages have gone down, economic growth is anemic, fuel and material costs are high, and we cannot afford what we once could. And not surprisingly, their years of fiddling, tinkering, and designing economical cars have paid off. Imports look better and better to increasing numbers of Americans, who have been pressed by the economy and now examine closely how they invest their hard-earned money. Ninety percent of Americans who buy Hondas say they would do so again. No U.S. car comes close to this level of consumer satisfaction except the Ford Escort, which contains foreign-built components assembled here.

The question is what should you, as someone dependent on the health of the U.S. auto industry, do? I have some suggestions, all related, that I hope will ensure that you, and your brother-in-law, have work far into the future.

First, don't just sit back as a union employee and get your information from the local. Set up a workers' committee at your own shop and start a dialogue with management. Find out the straight dope about your company. Is it sinking? Does it have negative cash flow? Is it living on borrowed time? What are its realistic prospects of surviving? Take part in discussions with management about what the company's weaknesses and strengths are. The antagonism between unions and management worked when profits were high, but it isn't worth a nickel if you lose your job. I can't tell you how to organize such discussions or even if management will listen, but somehow you, your fellow workers, and management have got to arrive at an understanding that your fates are common and that you must help each other. Precision Fabrication is a firm small enough to enable you to do this, and I am sure that there is a lot to be learned on both sides that would help everyone make better decisions. For Precision to survive, everyone must invest time and heart in the process.

Second, American car makers are finally getting serious about quality. They have to; their fate depends on it. And Precision's hope of gaining in a sinking industry is to be a quality leader. Over 60 percent of American cars are delivered to the dealer with defects. Any company that can institute the kind of quality that will allow General Motors' quality-control engineers to sleep at night will go to the top of the list. Although most of the problems with showroom defects are assemblage problems, the newer, longer warranties being offered will tell on brake hubs.

Third, remember that your competition in Japan, France, and Germany is being paid less than you are. In other words, your wages are too high. If you don't want them cut, you have to exceed foreign production rates. Realistically, I would compromise. Try to institute a program of wage cuts in return for worker equity.

Since Precision is in trouble, there have to be incentives on management's side to share the shrinking pie so that everyone will have a piece later. This is an ideal time for you and others to obtain not merely a wage but an actual portion of ownership that will reinforce, if the company is successful, your own retirement security.

The first thing you are going to say is that you can't do all this, that you don't know enough, and that you don't have the skills. Nonsense. You may not have sufficient skills, but no one else can do it for you. In fact, you have little choice. Either you are going to design your job for the future or you are going to be displaced. Unlike the past, when they burgeoned from the economy like fruit from a tree, jobs like yours will have to be carefully nurtured by workers. You have seen what management has done these past twenty years in the auto industry, so you know that management cannot be trusted to take into account everything it should in order to make your business work. You are the missing element in the success of American industry. If you want to sit on the sidelines, let the union bargain, and hope for the best, the insecurity that you feel at present will continue to gnaw at you and your family. To alleviate that feeling, take the initiative. The only way the American auto industry will recover is for thousands of people to be willing to examine honestly what is going on and change. You can only take care of your role in Precision—what you do does not guarantee the sale of Buicks. But your efforts will have their influence on others. There is an ocean between Japan and Detroit, but what is between a bad, good, and great car are the intangibles of care, craftsmanship, and motivation.

I have another suggestion. Industry observers in the Silicon Valley have discovered that of all the basic worker categories, machinists take to computers most easily. They don't know why but speculate that the

precision and mechanization of machine work is trans-
ferable to the understanding and operation of a computer. Despite all the talk about the information age,
the fact is that in industry, mechanization is still the
way things are made. This includes computers. In the
next decade, robotization is going to sweep through
the industry, and anything you do now to gain and
master computer technology and skills will put you in
an unusually strong position. Consider computers your
insurance. In the meantime, make Precision's business
your business.

Sincerely,
Paul Hawken

❋ Afterword

In the last week of October 1982, two seemingly unrelated articles appeared in the *Wall Street Journal* and *Business Week*. The first was a *Journal* editorial, "Energy Crisis Revisited," announcing that the energy crisis was over. In the second article, "Quality: The U.S. Drives to Catch Up," *Business Week* surveyed the revolution in U.S. business as management attempted to improve the quality of manufactured products.

The *Wall Street Journal* showed two different energy forecasts. The first was the Exxon/Shell/CIA model used in the mid-to-late seventies that projected inelastic energy demand clashing with limited supply, a forecast that would result in soaring energy prices. (See Figure 2.) The second model was a simple supply-and-demand curve, in which the rising price of a commodity lowers demand while simultaneously drawing forth more supplies. (See Figure 3.)

Figure 2

EXXON / SHELL / CIA FORECAST

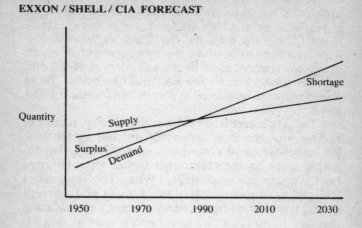

Figure 3

SUPPLY-AND-DEMAND CURVE (ECONOMICS 101)

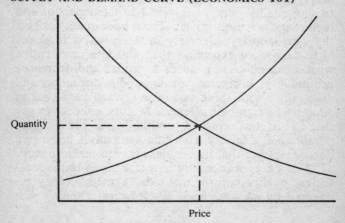

The *Journal* cited an editorial printed five years earlier that said the free market would solve the energy problem if left to its own workings. And so it has. Oil is available, demand has dropped, and prices are stable if not falling. But how did this happen? What has allowed nations to produce the same number of goods using less energy? How have consumers changed during this time? What have corporations done? These questions were answered in part by the *Business Week* piece.

The article reported evidence that quality, not price, had become the most important purchasing criterion for companies and consumers. Quality had also replaced price as the factor that would most improve market share and profitability. When a society places the quality of goods above the amount and price of goods, it is shifting from a mass economy emphasizing quantity to an informative economy emphasizing intelligence. This basic shift in manufacturing emphasis is due to two important considerations: the high cost of energy and the high cost of waste.

The U.S. automobile industry has estimated that nearly 25 percent of the cost of each car "is attributable to poor quality: scrappage, reject parts, inspection and repair, and warranty costs." Thus, poor quality affects the auto industry adversely in three ways: it makes U.S. cars more expensive than and less competitive with imported cars; it raises overhead and decreases profitability; it creates consumer dissatisfaction and disloyalty. With three out of every ten cars sold in America foreign-built, General Motors' executives say that quality has replaced profitability as the top corporate goal, a far cry from that company's boast two decades earlier that its business was to make money.

Many corporations are now starting to employ statistical quality control methods, a methodology pioneered by an American, W. Edwards Deming, but first implemented thirty years ago by Japanese companies; in turn, these companies are forcing their suppliers to take on similar quality control efforts. Xerox has promised its suppliers contracts that are good for the life of a product if the supplier will furnish parts with near-zero defects. Hewlett-Packard estimates that its quality control efforts will result in a 33 percent savings in manufacturing labor. Borg-Warner estimates that 20 percent of its product costs can be eliminated by a newly instituted quality control program.

How are quality and the "energy crisis" related? By the fact that the mass economy has grown for nearly one hundred years through the use of cheaper energy. This type of growth rewarded the rate, quantity, and scale of production, emphasizing the proliferation of goods as the means to profits, expansion, and power. To prosper in an economy where energy costs are rising entails an opposite approach to production, one in which the rate, quantity, and scale of production become subordinate to the care, quality, and utility of goods produced. Quality means the elimination of waste, which saves energy, and the elimination of waste is the essence of the meaning of the word *economy*.

We are in a contracting economy, but not the kind of contraction seen during the Great Depression or other times of economic displacement. We are in a natural, selective, and adaptive phase of contraction in which every aspect of the U.S. economy, from consumption to production, will be revolutionized, changed from the use of mass toward the increased use of intelligence, cooperation, and understanding. Although the supply-and-demand curve in Figure 3 is accurate in principle, a more discerning description of the gap between energy supply and demand once anticipated by forecasters would be one in which the gap was filled by more information. The rise and development of the informative economy could not have happened without the rise in energy prices. Now that it has begun, the process of increasing the ratio of information to mass in the production of goods and services cannot be stopped, no more than the Industrial Revolution could have been stopped. According to Joseph M. Juran, a quality control consultant who has worked with the Japanese since the early fifties, the change in American business practice toward quality is "unprecedented."

The *Wall Street Journal* stated that "high prices will draw forth more oil and its substitutes." The most important substitute for increased energy costs is the elimination of waste through improved quality and design. To create informatively made goods requires a complete change in the relationship among business, labor, and the consumer, because quality is not only a technique but an attitude—one that can only be sustained in the workplace by communication and understanding. In this light, the Ford Motor Company has recently instructed its managers to cease being authoritarian with employees and union members. Management is being sent to schools to learn how to be open and cooperative. Companies stressing quality have found that they must also initiate other programs including employee stock ownership programs, profit sharing, and shared decision making. Traditional forms of hierarchical control break down when the aim is to bring people together to accomplish a mutual goal or perfect a desired process. Economic survival requires a new set of rules.

I agree with the *Wall Street Journal*—there is no energy crisis. And there may never be one. There has been a crisis of perception, a lapse in our ability to see that our society and economy are almost infinitely flexible and adaptive to change. What the economy and the greater environment are telling us is to move to a more evolved economic structure. In the "next economy," virtually every product, process, and service will be completely redesigned and newly constituted.

We are about to remake our world once again, as we have been doing since the Industrial Revolution. The purpose of making society information-rich is to make it work effectively, efficiently, and economically. Remaking our world is not only our task, it is probably the greatest economic opportunity that has ever existed.

❧ Bibliography

Barnet, Richard J. *The Lean Years: Politics in the Age of Scarcity.*
New York: Simon and Schuster, 1980.

Braudel, Fernand. *The Structures of Everyday Life: Civilization and Capitalism, 15th to 18th Century*, vol. 1. New York: Harper & Row, 1981.

————. *Afterthoughts on Material Civilization and Capitalism.* Baltimore: Johns Hopkins University Press, 1977.

Brown, Lester. *Building a Sustainable Society.* New York: Norton, 1982.

Burns, Scott. *Home, Inc.: The Hidden Wealth and Power of the American Household.* Garden City, N.Y.: Doubleday & Co., 1975.

Casey, Douglas. *Strategic Investing.* New York: Simon and Schuster, 1982.

Cass, Roger. *The World Economy (1982)—The End of the Golden Age? Part 5—The International Liquidity Crisis.* Santa Barbara, Calif.: NAE Research Associates, Inc., May 1982.

Clark, Wilson. *Energy for Survival: The Alternative to Extinction.* Garden City, N.Y.: Anchor Books, 1974.

Commoner, Barry. *The Politics of Energy.* New York: Alfred A. Knopf, 1979.

Gilder, George. *Wealth and Poverty.* New York: Basic Books, 1981.

Hawken, Paul G.; Ogilvy, James; and Schwartz, Peter. *Seven To-morrows: Toward a Voluntary History*. New York: Bantam Books, 1982.

Heilbroner, Robert L. *The Worldly Philosophers: The Lives, Times and Ideas of the Great Economic Thinkers*. New York: Simon and Schuster, 1953.

Hubbert, M. K. "Energy Resources." In *Resources and Man*, edited by Preston Cloud. San Francisco: W. H. Freeman and Co., 1969.

Hughes, Jonathan. *Industrialization and Economic History, Theses and Conjectures*. New York: McGraw-Hill, 1970.

Johnson, Warren. *Muddling Toward Frugality: A Blueprint for Survival in the 1980s*. San Francisco: Sierra Club Books, 1978.

Keynes, John Maynard. *The General Theory of Employment, Interest, and Money*. New York: Harcourt, Brace & World, 1964.

Landes, David S. *The Unbound Prometheus: Technological Change and Industrial Development in Western Europe from 1750 to the Present*. Cambridge: At the University Press, 1969.

Lovins, Amory B. *World Energy Strategies: Facts, Issues, and Options*. San Francisco: Friends of the Earth; Cambridge, Massachusetts: Ballinger Publishing Co., 1975.

Masuda, Yoneji. *The Information Society as Post-Industrial Society*. Bethesda, Md.: World Future Society, 1981.

Morris, David. *Self-Reliant Cities: Energy and the Transformation of Urban America*. San Francisco: Sierra Club Books, 1982.

Naisbitt, John. *Megatrends: Ten New Directions Transforming Our Lives*. New York: Warner Books, 1982.

Ogilvy, James. *Many Dimensional Man: Decentralizing Self, Society, and the Sacred*. New York: Oxford University Press, 1977.

Ouchi, William. *Theory Z: How American Business Can Meet the Japanese Challenge*. Reading, Mass.: Addison-Wesley, 1981.

Porat, Marc. *Information Economy: Definition and Measurement*. Washington, D.C.: U.S. Department of Commerce, Office of Telecommunications, 1977.

Simon, Julian L. *The Ultimate Resource*. Princeton, N.J.: Princeton University Press, 1981.

Solomon, Ezra. *Beyond the Turning Point: The U.S. Economy in the 1980s*. San Francisco: W. H. Freeman and Co., 1981–82.

Thurow, Lester C. *The Zero-Sum Society: Distribution and the Possibilities for Economic Change*. New York: Basic Books, 1980.

Wendt, Lloyd. *The Wall Street Journal*. New York: Rand McNally & Co., 1982.

Wilson, John. *After Affluence: Economics to Meet Human Needs*. New York: Harper & Row, 1980.

 # Notes

Introduction

page

2   the "thrusting, restive search..." Heilbroner, Robert L., "Does Capitalism Have a Future?" *New York Times Magazine*, August 15, 1982.

Chapter 1. The Decline of the Mass Economy

page

13   the great items of trade: Heilbroner, Robert L., *The Worldly Philosophers*, pp. 20–39.

14   Thomas Newcomen perfected: Clark, Wilson, *Energy for Survival*, pp. 7–8, 29–33.

14   The impact of coal: Morris, David, *Self-Reliant Cities*, p. 55.

16   manufacturing horsepower quintupled: Clark, *Energy for Survival*, p. 55.

16   from 8,000 vehicles in 1900: Ibid., p. 40.

24   The period between 1950 and 1973: Solomon, Ezra, *Beyond the Turning Point*, p. 117.

25   This means that many jobs will be lost: "Work Force Shift Tied to Grimmer Jobless Impact," *New York Times*, August 13, 1982.

Chapter 2. The Rise of Oil

page

30   As early as 1950 came predictions: "Oil and Gas Resources: Did USGS Gush Too High?" *Science*, July 12, 1974.

30   A cartel depends on a single assumption: "Twilight Nears for the Age of Oil," *New York Times* Business Section, August 29, 1982.

31   In a mere twenty-year period: Solomon, Ezra, *Beyond the Turning Point*, p. 86.

31   The Yom Kippur War: Ibid., pp. 89–91.

33   productivity in the United States increased: Ibid., p. 117.

33   Between 1948 and 1966, worker productivity: Ibid., p. 117.

35   Since Simon's book was widely praised: Simon, Julian L., *The Ultimate Resource*, pp. 17–29.

36   two Cornell University scientists: "Increased Drilling for Oil May Consume More Energy Than It Gleans, Study Finds," *Wall Street Journal*, February 3, 1982.

39   New oil will be found: "Exotic New Technology Used in Oil Drilling Is Leading to Big Success, a Rise in Reserves." Ibid.

39   Between 1972 and 1974, the American energy industry: Commoner, Barry, *The Politics of Energy*, p. 29.

40   Oil currently provides one-half: "The World's Falling Need for Crude Oil," *Wall Street Journal*, April 21, 1981.

Chapter 3. Debt and Capital

page

48   While some of this debt: "No More Free Lunch for the Middle Class," *New York Times Magazine*, January 17, 1982.

56   Between 1950 and 1980 federal debt: Heller, Walter W., "Economic Rays of Hope," *Wall Street Journal*, December 31, 1980.

56   But debt has been increasing: Hulbert, Mark, "The Debtor Economy," *Challenge*, July–August, 1980.

57   As greater demands are placed: Ibid.

57   This rise in debt: Silk, Leonard, "Grim Reality of the Budget," *New York Times*, April 28, 1982.

59   Volcker's intention was to bring inflation: Blustein, Paul, "The Deficit Follies: 'What, Me Worry?'" *Wall Street Journal*, December 28, 1981.

59   As the economy continued to weaken: "Debt's New Dangers," *Business Week*, July 26, 1982.

60   In the words of a pessimistic governor: "Fed's Interest

Rate Dilemma," *New York Times*, June 15, 1982.

60   The last time the United States: Silk, Leonard, "Will History Repeat Itself?" *New York Times*, November 14, 1982.

60   The structure of debt: Heilbroner, Robert L., "Inflationary Capitalism," *The New Yorker*, October 8, 1979.

61   Merrill Lynch has an even better idea: "When Home Is a Line of Credit," *Business Week*, November 8, 1982.

Chapter 4. The Long Contraction

page

66   The case of the Manville Corporation: "Manville's Big Concern as It Files in Chapter 11 Is Litigation, Not Debt," *Wall Street Journal*, August 27, 1982.

68   But U.S. sales were: "Importers Take a Record Share of Car Market," *Wall Street Journal*, September 7, 1982.

68   The U.S. housing industry: "The Great Housing Collapse," *Newsweek*, March 29, 1982.

68   "It is the same phenomenon . . .": "Home Builders Expect a Persistent Slump with a Slow Recovery, Shrinking Industry," *Wall Street Journal*, February 8, 1982.

68   It is estimated that the Bank of America: Brooks, Andree, "Foreclosing on a Dream," *New York Times Magazine*, September 12, 1982.

69   The American steel industry: Chavez, Lydia, "The Year the Bottom Fell Out for Steel," *New York Times*, June 20, 1982.

69   With labor costs 50 percent higher: Chavez, Lydia, "Few Signs of Any Steel Upturn Seen," *New York Times*, September 8, 1982.

70   More ominous for long-term economic health: "A Jobs-Watcher Holds Little Hope for Quick Improvement," *New York Times*, September 5, 1982.

71   Now these works are wearing out: Herbers, John, "Alarm Rises over Decay in U.S. Public Works," *New York Times*, September 11, 1981.

71   The total bill over the next decade: Stall, Bill, "America Is Falling Apart," *San Francisco Chronicle*, November 26, 1981.

72   In contrast, if the assets: Rudnitsky, Howard, "On the Razor's Edge of a Financial Panic," *Forbes*, March 31, 1980.

72   Losses have also been incurred by: Burns, Scott, "Reading Between the Lines," *San Francisco Examiner and Chronicle*, March 15, 1981.

72   Against potential depositor losses: "How Safe Are Your Savings?" *Newsweek*, March 15, 1982.

72   At present the FSLIC: "The Thrifts' Physician: 'Dr. Doom,'" *Business Week*, May 24, 1982.

72   The FSLIC allows the solvent partner: "U.S. Expected to Cut Costly Efforts to Force Mergers of Troubled S&Ls," *Wall Street Journal*, February 17, 1982.

73   During the fifties and sixties, declining fuel prices: "A High-Risk Era for the Utilities," *Business Week*, February 23, 1981.

73   The utilities are caught: Parisi, Anthony, "Sunset for Nuclear Power," *San Francisco Chronicle*, "This World," April 26, 1981.

73   In order to maintain earnings growth: "Big Financial Problems Hit Electric Utilities; Bankruptcies Feared," *Wall Street Journal*, February 2, 1981.

74   Because many of the power plants: "Big A-Power Industry Bailout Plan Reported," *San Francisco Chronicle*, February 4, 1982.

74   A unique and fascinating way: Burns, Scott, "Over a Barrel," *San Francisco Sunday Examiner and Chronicle*, January 25, 1981.

76   The world has experienced: "Echoes from a Siberian Prison Camp," *Forbes*, November 9, 1982.

77   Forrester has joined with other economists: "A Technology Lag That May Stifle Growth," *Business Week*, October 11, 1982.

78   If Forrester's theory is correct: "A Black Cloud over the Smokestack Industries," *Business Week*, October 18, 1982.

79   Each of these periods was preceded: Lewis, Paul, "Boom-and-Bust Theory Shines like New," *New York Times*, October 17, 1982.

79   The total owed by developing nations: "Lenders' Jitters: International Bankers Take Steps to Restore Faith in Their System," *Wall Street Journal*, September 15, 1982.

79   This generous surge in lending: "Worry at the World's Banks," *Business Week*, September 6, 1982.

80   78 percent of Argentina's foreign earnings: "Third World Debt Crunch," *Newsweek*, June 7, 1982.

80–81   The banks, instead of acknowledging this dilemma: "The Crash of 198?," *The Economist*, October 16, 1982.

81   "The choice confronting governments . . .": Gall, Norman, "The World Gasps for Liquidity," *Forbes*, October 11, 1982.

81   Felix Rohatyn said outright: Rohatyn, Felix, "The State of the Banks," *New York Review of Books*, November 4, 1982.

82   As the worldwide recession has taken hold: "Threat of a Trade War Rises as Recession Spurs Competition, Na-

tions Impose Curbs," *Wall Street Journal*, November 17, 1982.

83   the problem of rising indebtedness: "Stagnation Facing World Economy, Warns BIS," *Financial Times*, June 15, 1982.

Chapter 5. The Informative Economy

page

87   sales of this printer quadrupled: "Quality: The U.S. Drives to Catch Up," *Business Week*, November 1, 1982.

88   Steelworkers are laid off: Cook, James, "The Molting of America," *Forbes*, November 22, 1982.

94   Village Homes, built and developed: Morris, David, *The New City-States*, Washington, D.C.: Institute for Local Self-Reliance, 1982, pp. 16–17.

96   When Ford succeeded Nixon: Solomon, Ezra, *Beyond the Turning Point*, pp. 100–101.

Chapter 6. Growth or Change?

page

103   The Mellon Institute estimates: "Energy Conservation: Spawning a Billion-Dollar Business," *Business Week*, April 6, 1981.

106   The shift of the mass economy: Dewar, A. J., paper delivered to Peter Schwartz, Royal-Dutch Shell, London, July 16, 1982.

112   Ecology is the study: Ogilvy, James, "Education, Evolution, and the Future," *Journal of Thought*, Fall 1981.

112   Part of this biological shortfall: Brown, Lester, "The Deterioration of the Economy's Environmental Support Systems," Washington, D.C.: Worldwatch Features, Worldwatch Institute, 1982.

114   By putting so much capital: "Farm Crisis Falls Short of Depression's Agony But There Are Parallels," *Wall Street Journal*, October 18, 1982.

116   The conclusion that small farms: "Smaller Is Better and Private Best for Farming," *New York Times*, March 21, 1982.

117–118 Uniroyal has created a council: "The Cooperative Economy," *New York Times*, February 14, 1982.

118   To cope with rapid economic change: "How Job Rotation Works for Japanese," *New York Times*, July 12, 1982.

Chapter 7. The Informative Strategy

page

120   Industrial technology that began with machines: Ohtsubo, Takebi, "Product Development Strategy in Japanese Industries," paper delivered at Nomura Research Institute Forum, June 1982.

123   Schlitz not only made: "The Perils of Cutting Quality," *New York Times*, August 22, 1982.

124   Eastern Airlines is famed: "Stuck in Old Technology." Ibid.

125   the Ruan Transport Company has designed: "The Million-Mile Truck Rolls In," *Business Week*, January 25, 1982.

126   Toshiba has produced a refrigerator: "Japanese Build a More Efficient Refrigerator," *Not Man Apart*, April 1982.

126   Several small companies now design: Fishman, Joanne A., "A Fresh Wind for Sail Power," *New York Times Magazine*, December 6, 1981.

128   the average age of cars on the road: "People Are Keeping Cars Longer as Costs Rise and Attitudes Change," *Wall Street Journal*, January 7, 1982.

128   the chairman of American Motors . . . has strongly advocated: "Why Detroit Is Not Selling Cars," *Business Week*, August 30, 1982.

128   While the American steel industry is reeling: "Mini-Mill Steelmakers, No Longer Very Small, Outperform Big Ones," *Wall Street Journal*, January 12, 1981.

129   this reaction to the rising costs: "The Underground Economy's Hidden Force," *Business Week*, April 5, 1982.

130   The informal economy is the individual's response: "The Underground—No Recession There," *New York Times*, July 4, 1982.

131   This type of work . . . called the "fourth sector": Heinze, Rolf G., and Olk, Thomas, "Development of the Informal Economy: A Strategy for Resolving the Crisis of the Welfare State," *Futures*, June 1982.

132   Pollster Louis Harris puts the figure: "Answers That Unveil the Underground Economy," *Business Week*, October 11, 1982.

Chapter 8. Disintermediation

page

134   gross world production climbed: Cass, Roger, *The World Economy (1982)—The End of the Golden Age? Part 5—The International Liquidity Crisis*, p. 13.

139   It includes all attempts: Illich, Ivan, *Vernacular Gender*,

Cuernavaca, Mexico: Valentina Borremans, 1982.

140   we have been told that nuclear energy: "Electricity Costs
       Rise Sharply as Utilities Add New Nuclear Facilities,"
       Wall Street Journal, August 14, 1982.

141   10 Btu per calorie of food: Clark, Wilson, "U.S. Agricul-
       ture Is Growing Trouble as Well as Crops," *Smithsonian*,
       January 1975.

142   a new product by Procter & Gamble: "In Spite of Huge
       Losses, Procter & Gamble Tries Once More to Revive
       Pringle's Chips," *Wall Street Journal*, October 7, 1981.

144   also corporations are seeking means: "New Alternatives
       to Litigation," *New York Times*, November 1, 1982.

145   Because there is a widespread belief: Levitt, Arthur, Jr.,
       "In Praise of Small Business," *New York Times Magazine*,
       December 6, 1981.

147   Arco stations, like all other gas stations: "Jockeying at the
       Pump," *Newsweek*, September 27, 1982.

148   Sometimes disintermediation is brought about by: "The
       Albacore Alliance/Local Fishermen Sell Catch Here for
       $1 a Pound," *Marin Scope*, October 5–11, 1982.

148   Another example of disintermediation in California: "With
       Housing Costs So High, More People Take on Trying Job:
       Building Own Homes," *Wall Street Journal*, September
       14, 1982.

148   Another kind of intermediation is the formation: "'Scle-
       rosis' Blamed for Economic Stagnation," *Science*, Octo-
       ber 1982.

Chapter 9. Seven Ways to Think About Your Money

page
153   In 1928 and 1929 Roger Babson: Wendt, *The Wall Street
       Journal* [book], p. 195.

156   If you invest in stocks: "Are More Chryslers in the Off-
       ing?" *Forbes*, February 2, 1981.

Chapter 10. The Next Economy

page
177   W. Earl Sasser, a professor at: "Quality: The U.S. Drives
       to Catch Up," *Business Week*, November 1, 1982.

178   Maytag, a maker of household appliances: "Maytag Re-
       pairmen May Soon Be Busy," *San Francisco Chronicle*,
       August 16, 1982.

181   Braudel, at seventy-nine, stated: "A Chat with Fernand
       Braudel," *Forbes*, June 21, 1982.

197 It is this faulty perception: "Exxon's Mining Unit Finds It Tough Going after 16 Years in Field," *Wall Street Journal*, August 31, 1982.

199 Mobil announced in fall 1982: "Exxon Leaves Dealers High and Dry," *New York Times*, September 8, 1982.

Afterword

page

210 The first was a *Journal* editorial: "Energy Crisis Revisited," *Wall Street Journal*, October 22, 1982.

210 Business Week surveyed the revolution: "Quality: The U.S. Drives to Catch Up," *Business Week*, November 1, 1982.

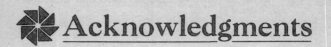# Acknowledgments

This book would not be complete without my acknowledging the many people who helped create it. It was Stewart Brand who coaxed these ideas into print. Throughout the writing of the book, his insight provided fresh paths and means of expression. Although I take responsibility for the flesh of the book, it was Stewart who gave it spine.

My agent, Joseph Spieler, is the kind authors dream of: diligent, literate, and dedicated. Joseph not only acted as interlocutor but also doubled as a tough and demanding editor. Authors would have a happier lot if all agents were like Joseph.

Peter Schwartz was pivotal to the book's inception. It was in an interview with Peter in 1977 that the idea of a shift from mass to information in products was first discussed, and it was from Peter that I borrowed the term "the mass economy." His reading of early drafts provided direction, criticism, and balance.

My editor at Holt, Jennifer Josephy, was a joy to work with; always helpful and relaxed, she was cheerful and direct under the tightest of deadlines. Without her early faith in the project, it could not have been accomplished.

Peter Coyote was exceptionally helpful, providing a sense of language that I could rarely live up to. His understanding of the book and its ideas were talismans that gave me heart.

Tom Mandel of SRI provided valued opinions of early drafts, giving up time in his busy schedule to check facts, find tables, and seek data. Other readers to whom I am very grateful are Lewis Richmond, James Ogilvy, Benjamin Campbell, John Wilson, Ene Riisna, and Wayne Van Dyck.

Richard Russell's newsletters were very helpful in formulating the thoughts on saving in Chapter 9.

Katherine O'Connell worked tirelessly as a researcher and played a key role in determining the book's makeup and content. Peggi Oakley, Janet McCandless, and Russ Hickman, of Sunflower Compositors, recorded draft after draft on their Xerox 860 Word Processor with dispatch, good cheer, and élan, proving that the "old" qualities of forthrightness and friendliness combine perfectly with the technologies of tomorrow.

To my partner, David Smith, and associates at our business, I want to say thank you for the six-month leave of absence and the forbearance in putting up with my frantic schedule.

To the following people, for thoughts spoken and unsaid, actions taken and received, for kindnesses shared but insufficiently acknowledged, I want to express my deepest gratitude: Daniel Welch, Margaret Hawken, Richard Graff, Art Kleiner, the staff at CQ,

Stephanie Mills, Jerret Engle, David Harris, Jeremiah Abrams, Roy Anderson, Tony Staffieri, Angelo Fiori, Robert Schwartz, John McQuown, Larry Lee, and Rodney Hoffman.

And, most particularly and especially, I wish to thank my wife Anna. I have yet to imagine a better human being.

# Index

About the Author

Paul Hawken is a writer, consultant, and businessman. He is the coauthor (with James Ogilvy, of SRI International, and Peter Schwartz, of Royal Dutch/Shell) of SEVEN TO-MORROWS: TOWARD A VOLUNTARY HISTORY. He is the economics editor of COEVOLUTION QUARTERLY, where many of the ideas in THE NEXT ECONOMY first appeared in print. He consults with government and industry and works extensively with foundations and nonprofit organizations. His company, Smith & Hawken, Ltd., manufactures high-quality tools. He lives on a farm in northern California with his wife, Anna, and their two children.

About the Author